THE CREATORS OF WINNIE the POOH

To my dearly beloved friends Lilian and Noel O'Neill.

THE CREATORS OF WINNIE the POOH

A A Milne and E H Shephard

Andrew Norman

WHITE OWL
AN IMPRINT OF PEN & SWORD BOOKS LTD
YORKSHIRE – PHILADELPHIA

First published in Great Britain in 2024 by
PEN AND SWORD WHITE OWL
An imprint of
Pen & Sword Books Ltd
Yorkshire – Philadelphia

ISBN 978 1 39906 423 1

A CIP catalogue record for this book is available from the British Library.

Typeset in Times New Roman 11/14.5 by
SJmagic DESIGN SERVICES, India.
Printed and bound in the UK by CPI Group (UK) Ltd, Croydon, CR0 4YY.

The Publisher's authorised representative in the EU for product safety is
Authorised Rep Compliance Ltd., Ground Floor, 71 Lower Baggot Street,
Dublin D02 P593, Ireland.
www.arccompliance.com

For a complete list of Pen & Sword titles please contact

PEN & SWORD BOOKS LIMITED
George House, Units 12 & 13, Beevor Street, Off Pontefract Road,
Barnsley, South Yorkshire, S71 1HN, England
E-mail: enquiries@pen-and-sword.co.uk
Website: www.pen-and-sword.co.uk

or

PEN AND SWORD BOOKS
1950 Lawrence Rd, Havertown, PA 19083, USA
E-mail: uspen-and-sword@casematepublishers.com
Website: www.penandswordbooks.com

FSC www.fsc.org MIX Paper | Supporting responsible forestry FSC® C013604

Contents

Family Tree

A. A. Milne

Relevant Family Tree

John Vine Milne 1845-1932 = Sarah Maria Heginbotham 1840-1921

- David Barrett Milne 1879 - 1942 = Constance Fawcett
- Kenneth John Milne 1881 - 1929 = Maud Innes
- Alan Alexander Milne 18 Jan 1882 - 31 Jan 1956 = Dorothy ('Daphne') de Sélincourt 22 Sept 1890 - Jan 1971
  - Christopher Robin Milne 21 Aug 1920- 20 Apr 1996 = Leslie Elizabeth de Selincourt 6 May 1924 – Sept 1996
    - Clare Milne June 1956- 27 Oct 2012

Dorothy ('Daphne') de Sélincourt

Relevant Family Tree

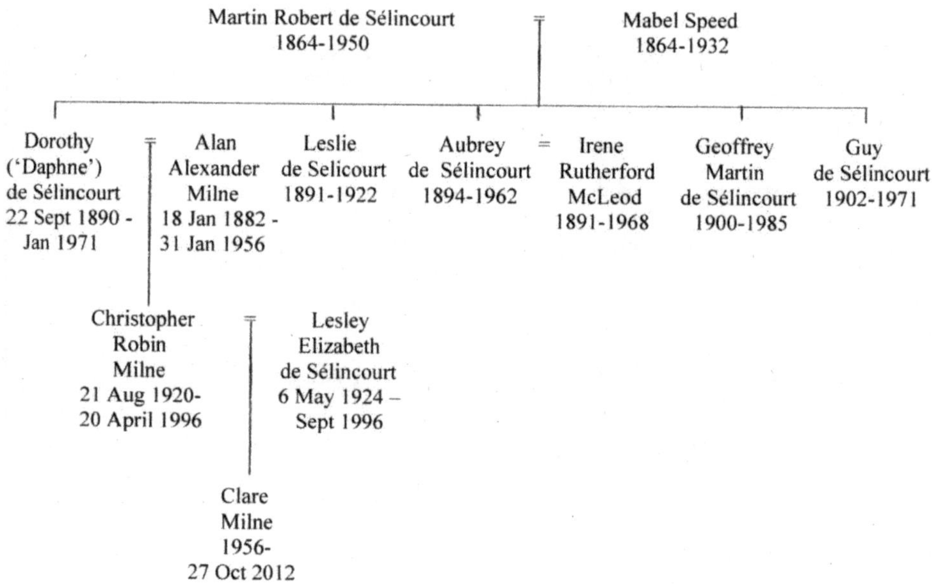

E. H. Shepard

Relevant Family Tree

Henry Dunkin Shepard 1845 -1902 = Harriet Jessie Lee 1854 -1890

- Cyril Harry Shepard 20 Dec 1877- 1 July 1916
- Ethel Jessie Shepard 1877-1947
- Ernest Howard Shepard 10 Dec 1879- 24 Mar 1976 (m1) = Florence Eleanor Chaplin 18 June 1876- 29 Sept 1927
  - Graham Howard Shepard 7 July 1907- 20 Sept 1943 = Anne Faith Gibbon 26 Aug 1907 - 2 Sept 1997
    - Harriet Jessie Minette Shepard 1937-
  - Eleanor Jessie Mary Shepard 25 Dec 1909 - 4 Sept 2000 = Edmund George Valpy Knox 1881- 1971

  (m2) = Norah Carroll 1903- 1977

Acknowledgements

I am grateful to the following: Scirard Lancelyn Green; Jo Maddocks, Assistant Curator of Rare Books, Weston Library, Bodleian Libraries, Broad Street, Oxford; Verity Parkinson, Resource Services & Support Librarian, Merton College, Merton Street, Oxford.

Preface

'Christopher Robin lived at the other end of the Forest, and when he came back with Rabbit, and saw the front half of Pooh, he said, "Silly old Bear", in such a loving voice that everybody felt quite hopeful again.'

Introduction

I woke up early in the morning, excited as it was my birthday. My mother Jean had made a cake with candles. My father Chris lit them with his cigarette lighter, and I blew them all out in one go. Whereupon my parents and my younger sister, Jane, applauded.

It was now time to open my presents. The first was from my grandfather Thomas: a Foden petrol tanker Dinky toy with dark blue cab, light blue body and real rubber wheels. The second, much to my delight, was from my uncle David, another Dinky toy, this time a dumper truck. I viewed my third and last present with suspicion. It was from my parents. Oh no, not another book, I thought. Why do they always give me books for my birthday and Christmas? Why not a cowboy outfit or a train set? I undid the wrapping and my worst fears were realised. *Now We Are Six*, said mother, reading the title aloud. 'We thought you'd like it dear, as it's your sixth birthday today.'

It was now evening and my bedtime. 'You haven't even looked at your book yet, Andrew', said mother reproachfully. 'No, mother.' 'Would you like me to read you a story from it? It's a book of poetry. Listen.' She began to read aloud in that sweet musical voice of hers and, within minutes, I found myself roaring with laughter at the exploits of Sir Thomas Tom, 'The Knight Whose Armour Didn't Squeak':

Of all the Knights in Appledore
The wisest was Sir Thomas Tom.
He multiplied as far as four,
And knew what nine was taken from
To make eleven. He could write
A letter to another Knight.[1]

I was already able to read the poems without the help of my parents, apart from the odd word, but better still, I loved my mother and father to read them aloud to me, when I was immediately transported into a magical world, featuring a bear named 'Pooh', who became by far the favourite fictional character of my early childhood, and his owner, 'Christopher Robin'. I recall feeling sorry for a little boy called 'Christopher Robin' who was about my age when he was ill in bed with 'Wheezles and Sneezles', but Pooh was the character I most wanted to hear about, and how I envied his owner!

And there is Pooh himself, giving his back a scratch; looking bemusedly at a blackboard full of sums; and finally following his owner, Christopher Robin up the stairs to bed!

It was obvious to me as a child that my parents enjoyed the poems as much as I did, and I subsequently wondered whether their author, A. A. Milne, and his wife Dorothy (known as 'Daphne') had a son. And if so, did he derive pleasure from them also? The answer was yes, and not only that, Milne's son was the real-life Christopher Robin.

Bears were clearly very much in the mind not only of Milne but of *Now We Are Six*'s illustrator Ernest Howard ('E. H.') Shepard. In fact, Shepard's illustration of the lovable bear occurs in no less than twelve of the thirty-five poems, and a total of sixteen times! Shephard was a genius, there is no doubt, for his illustrations perfectly reflect the warm and loving relationship between the bear and his owner.

As for Milne, in *Now We Are Six* he used the word 'bear' in only three of his poems, and only in two, namely 'Us Two' and 'The Friend', did he use the word 'Pooh'.

However, in two subsequent books, this time of short stories, entitled *Winnie-the-Pooh* (1926) and *The House at Pooh Corner* (1928), the eponymous fictional bear took centre stage!

In the poem 'Furry Bear', Pooh is looking at a real bear behind bars. This is significant, because it was from a real bear, which Milne and his son Christopher Robin encountered on their many visits to London Zoo, that Pooh derived his first name, 'Winnie', as will shortly be explained.

The lines of some of my favourite poems by Milne have stayed with me all my life. For example, I greatly appreciated 'The End' which, not surprisingly, is the final poem in *Now We Are Six*:

'When I was One,
I had just begun.
When I was Two,
I was nearly new.
When I was Three,
I was hardly Me.
When I was Four,
I was not much more.
When I was Five,
I was just alive.
But now I am Six, I'm as clever as clever.
So I think I'll be six now for ever and ever.'[2]

Many decades later, when Pooh became famous throughout the world, I re-read the poems and stories featuring a bear whose name evolved from being 'Teddy Bear' to 'Edward Bear', and finally to 'Winnie-the Pooh'. And I laughed just as uproariously as I had done all those years ago.

Up until then, it had never occurred to me to enquire about the author of the 'Pooh' poems and 'Pooh' stories, A. A. Milne, or about E. H. Shepard, the creator of the exquisite drawings of Pooh and his friends and of the bear's owner Christopher Robin that accompanied them. I now decided that it was time to put matters right. It was time to find out!

Chapter 1

Roger Lancelyn Green and the 'Golden Age' of Children's Books

Chapter 6 of *Essays and Studies*, published by John Murray in 1962, is headed 'The Golden Age of Children's Books'.[1] This phrase was coined by the author of the chapter, UK biographer and children's writer Roger Lancelyn Green (1918-1987). However, in coining the phrase, Lancelyn Green almost certainly had in mind Kenneth Grahame's book entitled, simply, *The Golden Age* (published in 1895).[2]

Lancelyn Green regarded the 'Golden Age' as just that. Grahame, however, used the term scathingly and cynically because, for him, childhood in the main was a time of utter estrangement between the child and its parents and adult relatives. In an account which appears to be at least in part autobiographical on Grahame's part, the narrator recounts his childhood in the company of his siblings Edward, Selina, Harold, and Charlotte. Referring to adults as the 'Olympians', Grahame acknowledged that yes, there was kindness, but otherwise:

'They treated us … with indifference', an indifference which was 'the result of a certain stupidity'. He had a 'vague sense' that some 'ruling power, wilful and freakish, and prone to the practice of vagaries' had given 'these hopeless and incapable creatures … authority over us … when it might far more reasonably have been given to ourselves over them'.

These Olympians, Grahame declared, seemed entirely oblivious to that which children find joyful. For example:

'For them the orchard (a place elf-haunted, wonderful!)' was simply there to produce 'apples and cherries. They never set foot within fir-wood or hazel-copse, nor dreamt of the marvels hid therein. The mysterious sources … that fed the duck-pond had no magic for them.'

Not only that, the Olympians had no imagination or sense of adventure:

'They were unaware of Indians, nor recked they anything of bisons or of pirates (with pistols!), though the whole place swarmed with such portents. They cared not about exploring for robbers' caves, nor digging for hidden treasure. Perhaps, indeed, it was one of their best qualities that they spent the greater part of their time stuffily indoors.'

Reck: pay heed to something.[3]

Grahame left his most scathing indictment of childhood, presumably as he had known it, to last:

'It was incessant matter for amazement how these Olympians would talk over our heads—during meals …. We illuminati, eating silently, our heads full of plans and conspiracies, could have told them what real life was. We had just left it outside, and were all on fire to get back to it.' Children, he said, were:

'One in thought and purpose, linked by the necessity of combating one hostile fate, a power antagonistic ever, — a power we lived to evade, — we had no confidants save ourselves. The estrangement was fortified by an abiding sense of injustice, arising from the refusal of the Olympians ever to defend, retract, or admit themselves in the wrong, or to accept similar concessions on our part.'

Finally, said Grahame, now that the Olympians 'are all past and gone … Somehow the sun does not seem to shine so brightly as it used … A saddening doubt, a dull suspicion, creeps over me. Can it be I too have become an Olympian?'[4]

Lancelyn Green suggested that his 'Golden Age' (which, it should be stressed, applied solely to the English-speaking world), commenced with two books by Charles Dodgson (pseudonym Lewis Carroll), namely *Alice's Adventures in Wonderland* (published in 1865) and *Through the Looking Glass* (published in 1871). Said he:

'Coming when they did, these two books revolutionized writing for the young. They captured the irresponsible fantasy in the minds of most children, and with it the unrealized urge toward rebellion against the imposed order and decorum of the world of the Olympians [Kenneth Grahame's euphemism for adults]….'[5]

Said US professor of English, Angela Sorby:

'The first Golden Age of children's literature, began, more or less, with *Alice in Wonderland* (1865) and ended with *Winnie-the-Pooh.*'.[6] A. A. Milne's two books featuring 'Winnie-the-Pooh', entitled *Winnie-the Pooh,* and *The House at Pooh Corner* were published in 1926 and 1928 respectively, Milne, together with E. H. Shepard who illustrated the two books, being the subject of this narrative. Milne's 'Winnie-the-Pooh' books were therefore published during the latter part of the period known as 'The Golden Age of Children's Books'.

Of the 'Golden Age' writers, Lancelyn Green gave the following a special mention: Rudyard Kipling, Kenneth Grahame J. M. Barrie; Beatrix Potter; Edith Nesbit; Frances Hodgson Burnett; and, of course, A. A. Milne.

In what way was *Alice's Adventures in Wonderland* considered to be so revolutionary?

Chapter 2

Alice's Adventures in Wonderland and the Dawn of the 'Golden Age' of Children's Books

Alice's Adventures in Wonderland proved to be a milestone in the canon of books for children, but in what way, and what opinion did A. A. Milne have of Charles Dodgson (aka Lewis Carroll)'s book?

Charles Dodgson: pseudonym Lewis Carroll

Author, poet, and mathematician Charles Lutwidge Dodgson was born on 27 January 1832 in Daresbury, Cheshire to father Charles, a country parson, and mother Frances Jane (née Lutwidge). He was the third oldest of 11 children.

Dodgson, who wrote poetry and short stories from a young age, became Lecturer in Mathematics at Christ Church College, Oxford. He was also an ordained deacon (minister of the Anglican Church). At Christ Church, Dodgson became close friends of Lorina, Edith, and in particular Alice, the three daughters of the Dean of Christ Church Henry George Liddell and his wife Lorina. All his life, Dodgson had suffered with a stammer, but in the company of the children, his stammer disappeared.

On 4 July 1862, Dodgson told a story to ten-year-old Alice, whereupon she begged him to write it down. It was finally published in 1865 as *Alice's Adventures in Wonderland*, having been illustrated by illustrator and political cartoonist Sir John Tenniel. This combination of author and illustrator made the book irresistible!

Alice's Adventures in Wonderland (published in 1865)

Principal characters

Human: Alice, heroine of the story; Queen of Hearts; King of Hearts; Knave of Hearts; the Duchess; the Hatter.

Anthropomorphic: the White Rabbit; Caterpillar; Cheshire Cat; March Hare; Dormouse; Gryphon; Mock Turtle.

Anthropomorphism: the attribution of human characteristics or behaviour to an animal.[1]

Setting

Wonderland, the abode of the King and Queen of Hearts and their court.

The story

Alice followed the White Rabbit, a messenger and a herald at the Court of the King and Queen of Hearts and found herself in Wonderland.

Alice's Adventures in Wonderland was a triumph, in terms of the mental agility, gymnastics, and acrobatics, and scintillating brilliance of the author. Not only that but the book changed the face of children's literature. In what way?

Dodgson allowed his heroine Alice to stand up and be counted; to take centre stage; to think 'outside the box'; to converse with 'grown-ups' on equal terms; to question them, and even to contradict them. At the same time, he entertained his child readers (and adults too!) with witty dialogue, interspersed with poems and songs.

> How doth the little crocodile
> Improve his shining tail
> And pour the waters of the
> Nile On every golden scale!
> How cheerfully he seems to grin,
> How neatly spreads his claws,
> And welcomes little fishes in
> With gently smiling jaws!

In fact, Dodgson encouraged children to question concepts, such as the making of assumptions, the nature of time, and how objects are defined. For example:

'"Have some wine," the March Hare said in an encouraging tone.

Alice looked all round the table, but there was nothing on it but tea. "I don't see any wine," she remarked.

"There isn't any," said the March Hare.

"Then it wasn't very civil of you to offer it," said Alice angrily.'

In respect of 'Time', said the Hatter, whom he regarded as a person:

"Now, if you only kept on good terms with him, he'd do almost anything you liked with the clock. For instance, suppose it were nine o'clock in the morning, just time to begin lessons: you'd only have to whisper a hint to Time, and round goes the clock in a twinkling! Half-past one, time for dinner!"

"That would be grand, certainly," said Alice thoughtfully: "but then — I shouldn't be hungry for it, you know."

"Not at first, perhaps," said the Hatter: "but you could keep it to half-past one as long as you liked."'

Finally, how did one define the 'Mock Turtle'? Said the Queen to Alice:

'"Have you seen the Mock Turtle yet?"

"No," said Alice. "I don't even know what a Mock Turtle is."

"It's the thing Mock Turtle Soup is made from," said the Queen.'

It was not until the very end of the book, that Dodgson introduced the word 'Wonderland'. Said he of Alice:

'So she sat on, with closed eyes, and half believed herself in Wonderland, though she knew she had but to open them again, and all would change to dull reality …'

Dodgson's motivation for writing the book

A. A. Milne had his own opinion of what motivated Dodgson to write his 'Alice' books:

'But don't suppose that this strange Lewis Carroll was now trying to amuse a world-audience, or that he was thinking, when once he had put pen to paper, of his Liddell girls. He was writing solely to amuse the strange Lewis Carroll, this childlike person whom he had suddenly discovered in himself.'[2]

A. A. Milne's opinion of Charles Dodgson and his works

Of Milne's opinion of Charles Dodgson, there is no doubt, for he was fulsome in his praise of the creator of 'Alice'. Writing in 1952 he described how:

'A fairy wand touched Don [Dodgson the Oxford don] and Deacon [Dodgson the Oxford deacon], and magically they became Lewis Carroll; the three little girls [daughters of the Dean] became magically a million little girls, a million little boys, big girls, big boys, men and women; and there was born on a golden afternoon nearly ninety years ago Alice, of Wonderland and the Looking Glass.' Had Dodgson:

'written no more than the *Snark* [*The Hunting of the Snark*, nonsense poem, published in 1876] and *The Walrus and the Carpenter* [narrative poem, published in 1871], he would have deserved immortality. But he would not have got it. He needed Alice to hold his hand. She is not pretty, as drawn by Tenniel [Sir John Tenniel, illustrator and satirical artist]; she has no great charm of manner; but, because she is a real child, wherever her piping voice is heard, children will follow, and at their heels will troop the grown-ups, eager to see what strange new company she is keeping. Look! Now she is talking to a man on a horse! Observe the spiked anklets round the horse's feet. That is to guard against the bites of Sharks. It is the rider's own invention ....'[3]

It was Milne's opinion, therefore, that Dodgson's 'Alice' books were to be enjoyed by both children and adults.

In what way did the writers of children's books from Lancelyn Green's 'Golden Age' break the mould, ignore the conventions of the time, and contrive to place children *at the very centre* of their stories? The truth is that they either omitted adults from them altogether, portrayed them as hostile or indifferent, or gave them roles that were merely supportive, as will now be seen.

Chapter 3

Some Male Authors from the 'Golden Age' of Children's Books

What was an author's motivation in writing a book which made him or her famous; how did they chose their subject matter; and most important of all, for whom were their books intended? Before directing these questions towards author A. A. Milne and illustrator E. H. Shepard, the twin subjects of this narrative, it is interesting to enquire briefly about some of the other principal authors of the 'Golden Age of Children's Books' - both male and female.

Rudyard Kipling

Novelist, writer, poet, and journalist Joseph Rudyard Kipling was born on 30 December 1865 in Bombay, India to father John Lockwood Kipling, Professor of Architectural Sculpture, and his wife Alice (née MacDonald).

At the age of 5, Kipling and his 3-year-old sister Alice were sent to stay with retired Merchant Navy captain Pryse Holloway and his wife Sarah at 4 Campbell Road, Southsea, Portsmouth, UK. Here, Kipling was desperately unhappy, describing 4 Campbell Road as the 'House of Desolation'.

At the age of 16, Kipling returned to Bombay where he became assistant editor and contributor of short stories to a newspaper. In 1889, after the publication of six collections of his short stories, Kipling returned to the UK. On 18 January 1892, he married US citizen Caroline Starr Balestier.

The couple subsequently settled in a property in Brattleboro, Vermont, USA, which they named 'Bliss Cottage'. Their first child Josephine was born on 29 December 1892. Here, Kipling wrote *The Jungle Book*, which was followed by a plethora of novels, short stories, and poems.

The Jungle Book (published in 1894)

Principal characters

Human: Mowgli, a human boy who was raised by wolves.

Anthropomorphic: Father Wolf and Mother Wolf (Mowgli's adoptive wolf parents); Tabaqui the jackal; Shere Khan the tiger; Bagheera the black panther.

Setting

India; the jungle.

The story

This is a tale of abandonment on the one hand, and kindness and compassion on the other.

Chapter I of *The Jungle Book*, entitled 'Mowgli's Brothers', begins as follows:

'It was seven o'clock of a very warm evening in the Seeonee hills when Father Wolf woke up from his day's rest, scratched himself, yawned, and spread out his paws one after the other to get rid of the sleepy feeling in the tips. Mother Wolf lay with her big gray nose dropped across her four tumbling, squealing cubs, and the moon shone into the mouth of the cave where they all lived. "Augrh!" said Father Wolf, "it is time to hunt again"; and he was going to spring downhill when a little shadow with a bushy tail crossed the threshold and whined: "Good luck go with you, O Chief of the Wolves; and good luck and strong white teeth go with the noble children, that they may never forget the hungry in this world." It was the jackal — Tabaqui.'

So here, immediately, Kipling introduces the concept of compassion – in this case, a concern for those with insufficient to eat.

Tabaqui now announced that:

'"Shere Khan, the Big One, has shifted his hunting-grounds. He will hunt among these hills during the next moon, so he has told me." Shere Khan was the tiger who lived near the Waingunga River, twenty miles away.'

'"He has no right!" Father Wolf began angrily. "By the Law of the Jungle he has no right to change his quarters without fair warning. He will frighten every head of game within ten miles; and I — I have to kill for two [i.e. himself and Mother Wolf], these days."'

'Father Wolf listened, and in the dark valley that ran down to a little river, he heard the dry, angry, snarly, singsong whine of a tiger who has caught nothing and does not care if all the jungle knows it. "The fool!" said Father Wolf. "To begin a night's work with that noise! Does he think that our buck are like his fat Waingunga bullocks?"'

'"H'sh! It is neither bullock nor buck that he hunts tonight," said Mother Wolf; "it is Man."'

Kipling's genius, in *The Jungle Book*, is to present the story not from the point of view of man, but from that of the animals of the jungle, who see man as the enemy. He also realised that conflict is at the heart of all good stories and here, it is not only man versus the animals but also the animals versus themselves.

'The Law of the Jungle, which never orders anything without a reason, forbids every beast to eat Man except when he is killing to show his children how to kill, and then he must hunt outside the hunting-grounds of his pack or tribe. The real reason for this is that man-killing means, sooner or later, the arrival of white men on elephants, with guns, and hundreds of brown men with gongs and rockets and torches. Then everybody in the jungle suffers.'

Man was therefore a potential threat to the jungle dwellers.

'The reason the beasts give among themselves is that Man is the weakest and most defenceless of all living things, and it is unsportsmanlike to touch him.' In other words, without the weaponry that man had developed, he would be no match for the jungle dwellers.

'"Something is coming uphill," said Mother Wolf, twitching one ear. "Get ready." The bushes rustled a little in the thicket, and Father Wolf dropped with his haunches under him, ready for his leap. Then, if you had been watching, you would have seen the most wonderful thing in the world — the wolf checked in mid-spring. He made his bound before he saw what it was he was jumping at, and then he tried to stop himself. The result was that he shot up straight into the air for four or five feet, landing almost where he left ground.

'"Man!" he snapped. "A man's cub. Look!"'

'Directly in front of him, holding on by a low branch, stood a naked brown baby who could just walk — as soft and as dimpled a little thing as ever came to a wolf's cave at night. He looked up into Father Wolf's face and laughed.'

'"Is that a man's cub?" said Mother Wolf. "I have never seen one. Bring it here."' She named the 'cub', who was a male, 'Mowgli'. He had been abandoned in the jungle and his parents had 'Run off'.

The outcome is that Mowgli was adopted by the wolf pack. The concept of a human being brought up by wolves is not new, as Kipling was surely aware. In Roman mythology, for example, twins Romulus and Remus were raised by wolves. However, a decade later, a change came about in Mowgli's thinking when he realised, albeit painfully, that he must return to humankind.

'"Now," he said, "I will go to men. But first I must say farewell to my mother"; and he went to the cave where she lived with Father Wolf, and he cried on her coat, while the four cubs howled miserably.'

'"Ye will not forget me?" said Mowgli.'

'"Never while we can follow a trail," said the cubs. "Come to the foot of the hill when thou art a man, and we will talk to thee; and we will come into the crop-lands to play with thee by night."'

'The dawn was beginning to break when Mowgli went down the hillside alone to the crops to meet those mysterious things that are called men.'

Kipling's motivation for writing the book

This question is easily resolved. In April 2010, Alison Flood, *The Guardian* newspaper's book reporter, stated as follows:

'A first edition of *The Jungle Book*, complete with a handwritten inscription by author Rudyard Kipling to his youngest daughter, has been discovered in a National Trust property in Cambridgeshire.'

The book is inscribed: "This book belongs to Josephine Kipling for whom it was written by her father. Tisbury. May 1894". Tisbury in Wiltshire was the home of Kipling's parents.

'The book was found in the library of Wimpole Hall in a collection belonging to Kipling's second daughter Elsie Bambridge, who lived in the property between 1938 and 1976. 'Josephine Kipling died of pneumonia aged six, five years after her father dedicated the book to her. Although the inscription is unsigned, the handwriting, based on analysis of many other items in the Kipling archive, is believed to be the author's.'[1]

Kipling, however, may have had an additional motive for writing *The Jungle Book*. The book is about abandonment, in the case of Mowgli, a similar abandonment to that which Kipling himself experienced when he and his sister were sent to Southsea, a distance of 4,500 miles as the crow flies from their family home in Bombay. The writing of the book may therefore have provided some kind of catharsis for its author Kipling.

Kenneth Grahame

Kenneth Grahame was born on 8 March 1859 in Edinburgh, Scotland to father James Cunningham Grahame, a lawyer, and his wife Elizabeth ('Bessie', née Ingles). He was the third of four siblings.

A few days after Grahame's fifth birthday and only weeks after giving birth to her fourth child Roland, Bessie died from scarlet fever at the age of 27. Cunningham now began drinking heavily, and in 1868 he abandoned the family and relocated to Calais, France. The outcome was that Kenneth and his siblings went to live with their maternal grandmother Mary Ingles, a widow, at her home 'The Mount', Cookham Dene, Berkshire. This gave Kenneth and his brother and soulmate William the opportunity to explore the nearby River Thames and its wildlife.

The two brothers were now enrolled at St Edward's Preparatory School in Oxford, where again Kenneth had the opportunity to explore the Thames. At St Edward's senior school, Kenneth excelled, becoming head boy and captain of rugby. However, in 1874, when Kenneth was aged 15, William died suddenly of an infection of the lungs.

Kenneth had hopes of going to Oxford University but for financial reasons was obliged to start work. In 1878, at the age of 19, he commenced as a clerk at the Bank of England, where he remained for over 30 years, rising to the exalted position of Secretary.

On 12 May 1899, Grahame married Elspeth (née Thomson), a socialite. However, he regretted having done so. As for Elspeth, that summer she wrote to Emma, wife of poet and novelist Thomas Hardy, for advice on her unhappy marriage. Emma's reply was not encouraging:

'I can scarcely think that love proper and enduring is in the nature of men — as a rule — perhaps there is no woman "whom custom will not stale".'[2]

On 18 May 1900 the couple's only child, Alastair, was born prematurely, with a cataract which left him blind in his right eye and with a severe squint in his left. His father affectionately nicknamed him 'Mouse'.

From the age of 4, Alastair was told bedtime stories by his father, and these stories came to feature 'Mr Toad', together with other characters including 'Rat', 'Badger', and 'Mole'. However, as he grew up, Alastair was plagued by ill health. Also, his behaviour became more and more bizarre:

'Once, when he wanted to see his father, who was in the bath at the time, he tried to break down the door; if 'Dutchy' (his German governess) crossed him, he was liable to kick her "about the body". And he was the terror of Kensington Gardens. He kicked and slapped little girls, digging "ten fingers deep into their tender flesh".'[3] In 1906 the Grahames relocated to Cookham Dene.

Is it possible to diagnose the illness from which Alastair has suffered from birth?

Congenital cataract often occurs in the offspring when the mother contracts German measles (rubella) in early pregnancy. Also, there is a correlation between Congenital Rubella Syndrome (CRS) and non-affective psychotic disorder – i.e. schizophrenia or a schizophrenia-type disorder, or a delusional disorder – and there is no doubt that Alastair was not of sound mind. Finally, there is a tendency for babies with CRS to be born prematurely, as was the case with Alastair. It is therefore likely that Alastair Grahame was a victim of CRS.

The Wind in the Willows (published in 1908)

Principal characters
Anthropomorphic: Otter; Toad; Mole; Rat; Badger.

Setting
'The River Bank'.

The story
Wealthy, jovial, kind-hearted, but impetuous and reckless Mr Toad was obsessed with dangerous pursuits, such as motoring at high speed. After numerous road traffic accidents, he repented of his wicked ways, was contrite, and agreed to compensate those he had wronged.

In Chapter I of *The Wind in the Willows*, Badger declares:

'There is no security, or peace and tranquillity, except underground. No builders, no tradesmen, no remarks passed on you by fellows looking over your wall, and, above all, no *weather* … No, up and out of doors is good enough to roam around and get one's living; but underground to come back to at last - that's my idea of *home*!'

Straightaway, therefore, the emphasis is on 'Home, sweet home'! As for Mole:

'He thought his happiness was complete when, as he meandered aimlessly along, suddenly he stood by the edge of a full-fed river. Never in his life had he seen a river before — this sleek, sinuous, full-bodied animal, chasing and chuckling, gripping things with a gurgle and leaving them with a laugh…. The Mole was bewitched, entranced, fascinated.'

So, here is the principal setting for the story, namely the River Bank.

Mole encountered the Water Rat, who invited him onto his boat to share his picnic:

'"This has been a wonderful day!" said he, as the Rat shoved off and took to the sculls again. "Do you know, I've never been in a boat before in all my life."'

'"Nice? It's the only thing," said the Water Rat solemnly as he leant forward for his stroke. "Believe me, my young friend, there is nothing — absolutely nothing — half so much worth doing as simply messing about in boats."'

Now, an element of danger is introduced:

'"What lies over there?" asked the Mole, waving a paw towards a background of woodland that darkly framed the water-meadows on one side of the river.'

'"That? O, that's just the Wild Wood," said the Rat shortly. "We don't go there very much, we river-bankers."'

'"And beyond the Wild Wood again?" he asked …'

'"Beyond the Wild Wood comes the Wide World," said the Rat. "And that's something that doesn't matter, either to you or me. I've never been there, and I'm never going, nor you either, if you've got any sense at all. Don't ever refer to it again, please."'

Otter appeared on the scene, and also Badger.

'When they got home, the Rat made a bright fire in the parlour, and planted the Mole in an arm-chair in front of it, having fetched down a dressing-gown and slippers for him, and told him river stories till supper-time.'

Here again, Grahame emphasises the delights and comforts of home. And now, Rat entertains with a song, one that he has composed about 'his friends, the ducks' and entitled 'Duck's Ditty':

> All along the backwater,
> Through the rushes tall,
> Ducks are a-dabbling,
> Up tails all!

Toad made his entrance and was scornful of the exploits of Mole and Rat on the river.

'"O, pooh! boating!" interrupted the Toad, in great disgust. "Silly boyish amusement. I've given that up long ago. Sheer waste of time, that's what it is. It makes me downright sorry to see you fellows, who ought to know better, spending all your energies in that aimless manner.'

Toad now showed his friends his newly-acquired gipsy caravan, which finished up in the ditch when a motor car appeared! Toad now acquired a succession of seven motor cars, all of which he crashed.

Meanwhile, when Mole got lost in the snow, Ratty came to the rescue. As for Toad,

'"He's been in hospital three times," put in the Mole; "and as for the fines he's had to pay, it's simply awful to think of."'

'"Yes, and that's part of the trouble," continued the Rat. "Toad's rich, we all know; but he's not a millionaire. And he's a hopelessly bad driver, and quite regardless of law and order. Killed or ruined — it's got to be one of the two things, sooner or later. Badger! We're his friends — oughtn't we to do something?"'

Toad was arrested and sentenced to twenty years in prison. However, he escaped disguised as a washerwoman! Meanwhile, when Otter's son Little Portly disappeared, Mole and Rat went out in a boat into the night in search of him.

Finally, Badger, aided by Mole, Rat, and Toad, drove out the Stoats and Weasels, who had taken over Toad's stately home, 'Toad Hall'.

When Toad repented of his reckless behaviour, he promised that:

'"Henceforth I will be a very different Toad. My friends, you shall never have occasion to blush for me again. But, O dear, O dear, this is a hard world!" And, pressing his handkerchief to his face, he left the room, with faltering footsteps.'

The theme of *The Wind in the Willows* is therefore the importance of the home, of hospitality, of good fellowship, and of caring for one another.

For example, despite the transgressions of Toad, his friends do not abandon him.

Grahame's motivation for writing the book

It was Grahame's habit to tell his son Alastair bedtime stories of his own creation. However, in May 1907, shortly before Alastair's seventh birthday Grahame and Elspeth took a prolonged holiday in Cornwall, leaving their son in the care of his nanny. Meanwhile, it was arranged for Alastair to go on holiday to Littlehampton [in West Sussex] with his new nursery governess ('Dutchy' having been replaced by Miss Naomi Stott). Whereupon Alastair 'refused point-blank because he would miss the adventures of Toad. He was persuaded only by his father's promise that further instalments would be sent by post, and so the letters began.'[4] To these letters, Grahame occasionally added little sketches.

The first letter, sent from the Green Bank Hotel, Falmouth, Cornwall, is dated 10 May 1907. It begins:

'My darling Mouse. This is a birthday letter to wish you very many happy returns of the day [Alastair's birthday would fall on the 18th of May]. I wish we could have been all together but, we shall meet again soon, & then we will have treats. I have sent you two picture books, one about Brer Rabbit, from Daddy, & one about some other animals, from Mummy.'[5] Surely this letter is indicative of the Grahames' love for their son.

Grahame's letter to Alastair, dated 21 June 1907, indicated that his holiday with Elspeth was over. The letter was posted from 16 Durham Villas, London. This:

'had been the Grahames' home for the first six years of their marriage and, following their move to Cookham Dene in 1906, was retained as a pied-à-terre.'[6]

Grahame's letter to Alistair dated 17 July 1907 began, 'My dear Robinson'. 'This followed Mouse's announcement that he was changing his name to Michael Robinson – a far finer name, he claimed, than Alistair Grahame.'[7] From now on, in regard to the letters sent by Grahame to Alastair, there were no friendly preambles, and each one ended simply 'To be continued'.

The final letter, which was dated 'Sept 1907', was headed 'Dear Robinson' in the same perfunctory way, before Grahame launched immediately into the story: 'The toad rather suspected what he was after, & did his best to get away …'. And it ends abruptly, at the end of the story, with not even a 'to be continued', or 'Your affectionate Daddy', as with the early 'pre-Robinson' letters.

These letters, of which there were fifteen in all, formed the basis of Grahame's novel *The Wind in the Willows*, which was published the following year. This had been at Elspeth's suggestion.

In a letter to his London publisher Methuen, Grahame indicated that he was thinking of a wider audience for *The Wind in the Willows*, which he described as:
'A book of Youth – and so perhaps chiefly *for* Youth, and those who still keep the spirits of youth alive in them: of life, sunshine, running water, woodlands, dusty roads, winter firesides; free of problems, clean of the clash of sex; of life as it might fairly be supposed to be regarded by some of the wise small things "that glide in grasses and rubble of woody wreck".' This is a quotation from the poem *Melampus* by George Meredith.[8]

In other words, Grahame had not only kept his son Alastair amused and entertained by his tales of 'Mr Toad', but in creating *The Wind in the*

Willows he had also relived a time of his own childhood, perhaps the only time of his life when he had been truly happy, and now it was to be shared with the wider world.

Finally, Grahame's reference to 'the clash of sex' may reflect a dislike on his part for sexual intercourse, which was evidently the reason for discord within his marriage.

A. A. Milne and E. H. Shepard, the subjects of this narrative, both waxed lyrical about *The Wind in the Willows*. In 1919 Milne stated:

'Should I ever find myself in the dock, and one never knows, my answer to the question whether I had anything to say would be, "Well, my lord, if I might just recommend a book to the jury before leaving". I shall not describe the book, for no description would help it. But I shall just say this; that it is what I call a Household Book. By a Household Book I mean a book which everybody in the household loves and quotes continually ever afterwards; a book which is read aloud to every new guest, and is regarded as the touchstone of his worth. But it is a book which makes you feel that, though everybody in the house loves it, it is only you who really appreciate it at its true value, and that the others are scarcely worthy of it. It is obvious, you persuade yourself, that the author was thinking of you when he wrote it.'[9]

In 1930 E. H. Shepard, who had previously illustrated A. A. Milne's Winnie-the-Pooh books, was commissioned to illustrate a new edition of

Kenneth Grahame's *The Wind in the Willows* and declared:

'I hesitated, as I considered it so perfect a work of art in itself that no pictures could do justice to it, but I learnt that it had been illustrated already by various artists, none of whom, to my mind, had made a success of it. I suppose I felt I could do better than this, anyway, I could try.'[10]

'Before undertaking the task, Shepard visited Grahame, then in his seventies.' This was at the author's house at Pangbourne in Berkshire. 'Grahame said to him, "I love these little people [Toad, Mole, Rat, Badger, etc], be kind to them'.[11]

'When I had made some drawings for the book', Shepard continued, 'I took them to Pangbourne'. Whereupon Grahame:

'was critical but I think he was pleased with my efforts and when he handed the drawings back to me he said, "I'm glad you've made them [Toad, et al] real". I always regret that he did not live long enough to see the new edition completed. The illustrations were a huge success, and have never been out of print.'[12]

J. M. Barrie

James Matthew Barrie was born on 9 May 1860 at Kirriemuir, Angus, Scotland to father David, a weaver, and his wife Margaret (née Ogilvy). Barrie was the 9th of 10 children, two of whom died before he was born.

***Peter Pan, or the Boy Who Wouldn't Grow Up* (staged as a play in December 1904; *Peter Pan in Kensington Gardens*, published in 1906; *Peter Pan and Wendy*, published in 1911).**

Principal characters
Human: Peter Pan, a boy who never grows up and the leader of the Lost Boys, who has the ability to fly; Wendy Darling, who was fond of Peter; the Lost Boys, who come to live in Neverland; Tinker Bell, a fairy and Peter's best friend; Captain Hook, Captain of the Pirates and Peter's nemesis; Redskins, a tribe of North American Indians who are at war with Captain Hook.

The Fairies: allies of the Lost Boys against the Pirates.
The Crocodile: Captain Hook's nemesis.

Setting
'Neverland' (an island).

The story
As infants, the Lost Boys were lost to their parents when they fell out of their perambulators. In Neverland, they have adventures involving pirates, mermaids, and Indians.

J. M. Barrie's motivation for writing the book.

People have speculated, ever since the book's publication, about the real meaning behind *Peter Pan*, and what inspired Barrie to write it.

The day before his 14th birthday, Barrie's older brother David died in an ice-skating accident. That was in the year 1866 and Barrie was aged 6 at the time. Whereupon, their mother Margaret withdrew herself for a prolonged period and clung on to David's christening gown.

In his memoir of his late mother, entitled *Margaret Ogilvy by Her Son*, Barrie described how one of his sisters told him to go to his mother:

'and say to her that she still had another boy. I went ben [indoors] excitedly, but the room was dark, and when I heard the door shut and no sound come from the bed I was afraid, and I stood still. I suppose I was breathing hard, or perhaps I was crying, for after a time I heard a listless voice that had never been listless before say, "Is that you?" I think the tone hurt me, for I made no answer, and then the voice said more anxiously "Is that you?" again. I thought it was the dead boy she was speaking to, and I said in a little lonely voice, "No, it's no him, it's just me." Then I heard a cry, and my mother turned in bed, and though it was dark I knew that she was holding out her arms.'[13]

Barrie was understandably horrified and bewildered by this lack of response from his mother Margaret (who died on 3 September 1895). Surely this why he wrote *Peter Pan*; the story of a group of boys, led by Peter, who have become separated from their parents, a story that parallels Barrie's own rejection by his mother! For now, in Neverland, at least Peter and the Lost Boys could enjoy an infinitely long childhood, spent in each other's company. But how could *they* cope without a mother?

In Chapter III of *Peter Pan*, Peter tells Wendy that he never receives letters.

'"But your mother gets letters?"

"Don't have a mother," he said. Not only had he no mother, but he had not the slightest desire to have one. He thought them very over-rated persons. Wendy, however, felt at once that she was in the presence of a tragedy.

"O Peter, no wonder you were crying," she said, and got out of bed and ran to him.

"I wasn't crying about mothers," he said rather indignantly. "I was crying because I can't get my shadow to stick on. Besides, I wasn't crying."'

Surely this is Barrie, vicariously through Peter Pan, bewailing the fact that, to all intents and purposes, he had no mother, and trying to disguise from her the pain that he was feeling in consequence.

In the story, but sadly not in Barrie's own life, there was a resolution of the problem. In Chapter VI when the Lost Boys build Wendy a house:

'"Lovely, darling house," Wendy said, and they were the very words they had hoped she would say.

"And we are your children," cried the twins.

Then all went on their knees, and holding out their arms cried, "O Wendy lady, be our mother."

"Ought I?" Wendy said, all shining. "Of course it's frightfully fascinating, but you see I am only a little girl. I have no real experience."

"That doesn't matter," said Peter, as if he were the only person present who knew all about it, though he was really the one who knew least. "What we need is just a nice motherly person."

"Oh dear!" Wendy said, "you see, I feel that is exactly what I am."

"It is, it is," they all cried; "we saw it at once."

"Very well," she said, "I will do my best. Come inside at once, you naughty children; I am sure your feet are damp. And before I put you to bed I have just time to finish the story of Cinderella."'

So, in the story at least, for Peter and the Lost Boys, the problem of having no mothers was solved.

Chapter 4

Some Female Authors from the 'Golden Age' of Children's Books

Beatrix Potter

Writer, illustrator, and natural scientist Helen Beatrix Potter was born on 28 July 1866 at West Brompton, London, to father Rupert W. Potter, a lawyer, and his wife Helen (née Leech). Beatrix had one sibling, a younger brother Bertram. As children, Beatrix and Bertram kept numerous small animals as pets. In 1882, Beatrix spent her first summer holiday with her family in the Lake District. Other holidays were taken in Scotland.

In the 1890s, Beatrix printed Christmas cards of her own design featuring mice and rabbits. In 1900, she privately published a story of hers about four little rabbits.

The Tale of Peter Rabbit (published in 1902)

Principal characters
Human: Mr McGregor.

Anthropomorphic: Peter Rabbit, and his siblings Flopsy, Mopsy, and Cotton-tail; their mother 'Old Mrs Rabbit'.

Setting
Mr McGregor's vegetable garden.

The story
The theme of *The Tale of Peter Rabbit* is the thrill of Peter being naughty and disobedient, and its rewards, but also its consequences:

'Once upon a time there were four little Rabbits, and their names were — Flopsy, Mopsy, Cotton-tail, and Peter. They lived with their Mother in a sand-bank, underneath the root of a very big fir-tree.'

Like all good mothers who are concerned for the welfare of their children, 'Old Mrs Rabbit' gave her four offspring some advice:

'Now my dears, you may go into the fields or down the lane, but don't go into Mr McGregor's garden: your Father had an accident there; he was put in a pie by Mrs. McGregor.'

Here is a stark warning, for all children of that era would have been familiar with rabbit pie, and known what it was made of!

'Flopsy, Mopsy, and Cotton-tail, who were good little bunnies, went down the lane to gather blackberries. But Peter, who was very naughty, ran straight away to Mr McGregor's garden, and squeezed under the gate! First he ate some lettuces and some French beans; and then he ate some radishes; and then, feeling rather sick, he went to look for some parsley.'

Beatrix has set the stage. Peter had been disobedient, and Beatrix's child readers would have wondered, would there be consequences for his bad behaviour? Sure enough, there are consequences because:

'round the end of a cucumber frame, whom should he meet but Mr McGregor!'

Peter now underwent a series of misfortunes as he was pursued hotfoot by a rake-wielding Mr McGregor. First, he lost one of his shoes, and then the other. Finally, when he was caught up in a gooseberry net, he lost his 'blue jacket with brass buttons', which was 'quite new'. In consequence, he found himself 'out of breath and trembling with fright'.

'Peter gave himself up for lost, and shed big tears.' As for Mr McGregor, he 'hung up the little jacket and the shoes for a scare-crow to frighten the blackbirds.' Finally, 'Peter never stopped running or looked behind him till he got home to the big fir-tree.' And now came the consequences.

'I am sorry to say that Peter was not very well during the evening. His mother put him to bed, and made some camomile tea; and she gave a dose of it to Peter! "One table-spoonful to be taken at bed-time.". But Flopsy, Mopsy, and Cotton-tail had bread and milk and blackberries for supper.'

Beatrix's motivation for writing the book

Beatrix was educated by a governess, and she therefore lacked the company of schoolfellows. Instead, her pets became her companions.

Although Beatrix grew up to have a 'no-nonsense' reputation, at heart she was a kind and compassionate person. From the Lake District and Scotland, she sent illustrated 'picture letters' to the children of her former governess Annie Carter Moore, and in particular to Annie's son Noel, who suffered with frequent bouts of illness. One of these stories, sent to Noel in September 1893, was published subsequently in 1902 as the aforementioned *The Tale of Peter Rabbit*, by London publisher Frederick Warne. This was the first of many published 'Tales' by Beatrix.

Beatrix was something of a rarity amongst authors in that she not only wrote her 'Tales' for children, she also illustrated them. For example, we see Peter enjoying two delicious carrots; being hotly pursued by Mr McGregor; and 'trembling with fright'! And Beatrix knew exactly how to engage children, with this tale of childhood – or in this case 'rabbithood', including disobedience, danger, pursuit, and the satisfaction that Peter had 'got away with it', albeit at a cost.

Furthermore, one may imagine Beatrix thinking, as she created, with loving care, *The Tale of Peter Rabbit*, 'I do hope that Noel will enjoy this, and hopefully feel better soon'. Noel and his siblings would surely have been enthralled by the story, as children throughout the world have been enthralled with it ever since!

Edith Nesbit

Writer and poet Edith Nesbit was born in 1858 in Kennington, London, to father John Collis Nesbitt, an agricultural chemist, and his wife Sarah (née Alderton). Edith was the youngest of a family of six, one of whom died in infancy.

Edith's father died in 1862 at the age of 43, when she was only 3 years old. Edith's sister Mary suffered from tuberculosis so the family relocated to

Europe in search of sea air and a milder climate, which was believed to be therapeutic. The family returned to England in 1870 and after Mary's death the following year, settled at Halstead Hall in Kent. Finally, the Nesbits were obliged, for financial reasons, to relocate to a modest house in London.

In 1880 Edith married journalist and socialist Hubert Bland, who lost his capital through making unwise investments. Both he and Edith were now obliged to write in order to support their growing family. Of all Edith's books, *The Railway Children* has always been a children's favourite.

The Railway Children (published in 1905)

Principal characters
Siblings Roberta, Peter, and Phyllis, and their parents Charles and Mrs Waterbury.

Setting
The steam railway.

The story
The middle-class Waterbury family was forced to relocate from London to the country and a life of poverty, following the wrongful arrest and imprisonment of their father on a charge of being a spy.

Twin themes of the story are stoicism and kindness: the stoicism that Mrs Waterbury displayed in her determination to support her children; the kindness of the children to stationmaster Albert Perks; to a passenger on the train, an elderly man who becomes the family's benefactor and who assists in the release from prison of Mr Waterbury; and the kindness of the family to a Russian exile who was formerly incarcerated in a Siberian prison camp; and to an injured schoolboy.

Edith's motivation for writing the book

Jessica Winter, editor at *The New Yorker*, summed this up succinctly. *The Railway Children*, she said, was:

'constructed from a blueprint that is also a kind of re-enactment of the author's own childhood: an idyll torn up at its roots by the exigencies of illness, loss, and grief.'[1]

Mrs Waterbury was therefore a reincarnation of Edith's mother Sarah, both displaying the same stoicism, perseverance, and determination to afford their children the best care possible despite their straightened circumstances. Finally, the theme of kindness to others, which is so evident in *The Railway Children*, chimes perfectly with Edith's socialist philosophy.

Frances Hodgson Burnett

British-US novelist and playwright Frances Hodgson Burnett was born on 24 November 1849 in Cheetham Hill, Manchester, UK to father Edwin Burnett, a supplier of fittings for the home such as chandeliers and brass door knockers, and his wife Eliza (née Bond). Frances was the third of five children.

In 1853, when Frances was only 4 years old, her father Edwin died. The family subsequently fell on hard times, and in 1865 the Burnetts emigrated to New Market, Tennessee, USA. This was at the invitation of an uncle. To earn money, Frances wrote stories for US magazines.

In 1873 Frances married US citizen Swan Burnett, who was shortly to qualify as a physician. The couple had two sons, Lionel, born the following year, and Vivian who was born in 1876 when the Burnetts relocated to Paris for two years. On their return, the Burnetts set up home in Washington DC.

In the 1880s Frances, who for much of her life suffered from depression, began to make a series of visits to England. In 1886 her novel *Little Lord Fauntleroy* was published. In 1898, she and Burnett divorced.

From 1898 Frances resided at Great Maytham Hall, Kent, UK, with its walled gardens and rose garden. This inspired her to write *The Secret Garden*. In February 1900, Frances married Stephen Townsend but the marriage ended two years later. In 1890, her eldest son Lionel died from tuberculosis.

The Secret Garden (published in 1911)

Principal characters

Mary Lennox (aged 10); her uncle Archibald Craven; her uncle's son Colin (aged 10); Martha, the chambermaid; Martha's brother Dickon (aged 12).

Setting

Misselthwaite Manor and its Secret Garden.

The story

Mary Lennox, a little girl living with her parents in India, realised that she was unwanted.

'Her father had held a position under the English Government and had always been busy and ill himself, and her mother had been a great beauty who cared only to go to parties and amuse herself with gay people. She had not wanted a little girl at all, and when Mary was born she handed her over to the care of an Ayah [nanny], who was made to understand that if she wished to please the Mem Sahib [Mary's mother] she must keep the child out of sight as much as possible.'

And now, following an outbreak of cholera in the family, Mary found herself an orphan:

'"I fell asleep when every one had the cholera and I have only just wakened up. Why does nobody come?" It was in that strange and sudden way that Mary found out that she had neither father nor mother left; that they had died and been carried away in the night, and that the few native servants who had not died also had left the house as quickly as they could get out of it, none of them even remembering that there was a Missie Sahib.'

Having been sent to England to live with her uncle Mr Archibald Craven at Misselthwaite Manor on his Yorkshire Estate, Mary experienced callousness and indifference from the housekeeper Mrs Medlock who, referring to her uncle told her:

'You needn't expect to see him, because ten to one you won't. And you mustn't expect that there will be people to talk to you. You'll have to play about and look after yourself. You'll be told what rooms you can go into and what rooms you're to keep out of. There's gardens enough. But when you're in the house don't go wandering and poking about. Mr. Craven won't have it.'

This is a throwback to the attitude prevalent in the pre-Golden Age when children were to be seen and not heard! However, Mary was made of sterner stuff! So, Frances has sowed the seed in her readers' minds: will Mary defy Mrs Medlock, and if so, what will the outcome be?

Martha, the chambermaid, told Mary about her brother:

'Our Dickon goes off on th' moor by himself an' plays for hours. That's how he made friends with th' pony. He's got sheep on th' moor that knows him, an' birds as comes an' eats out of his hand. However little there is to eat, he always saves a bit o' his bread to coax his pets.'

Surely this was the author, reflecting on her own deep and abiding love for the natural world. Now came Mary's first acquaintance with 'The Secret Garden':

'And then she took a long breath and looked behind her up the long walk to see if any one was coming. No one was coming. No one ever did come, it seemed, and she took another long breath, because she could not help it, and she held back the swinging curtain of ivy and pushed back the door which opened slowly — slowly. Then she slipped through it, and shut it behind her, and stood with her back against it, looking about her and breathing quite fast with excitement, and wonder, and delight. She was standing inside the secret garden.'

When Mary introduced Dickon, and her uncle Craven's son Colin who had always been treated as an invalid, to the Secret Garden, the effect on the latter was astonishing:

'And the sun fell warm upon his face like a hand with a lovely touch. And in wonder Mary and Dickon stood and stared at him. He looked so strange and different because a pink glow of color had actually crept all over him — ivory face and neck and hands and all.'

'"I shall get well! I shall get well!" he cried out. "Mary! Dickon! I shall get well! And I shall live forever and ever and ever! I shall stop being queer," he said, "if I go every day to the garden. There is Magic in there — good Magic, you know, Mary. I am sure there is."'

"So am I," said Mary.

"Even if it isn't real Magic," Colin said, "we can pretend it is. Something is there — something!"'

In fact, the word 'Magic' occurs no less than ninety-six times in the story! (Magic: the power of apparently influencing events by using mysterious or supernatural forces.[2])

Colin firmly believed that it was Mary and Dickon and their special powers that had brought about his recovery, together with his own efforts:

'I had to try myself at the same time, of course, but her Magic helped me — and so did Dickon's. Every morning and evening and as often in the daytime as I can remember I am going to say, "Magic is in me! Magic is making me well! I am going to be as strong as Dickon, as strong as Dickon!" I am sure there is Magic in everything, only we have not sense enough to get hold of it and make it do things for us — like electricity and horses and steam.' This is the theory of 'Mind over Matter' – an idiom 'used to describe a situation in which someone is able to control a physical condition, problem, etc., by using the mind'.[3]

The Secret Garden was therefore not only a source of delight to the three children, but because of 'the spell' which Mary 'had worked', it was a place where they all grew healthier and stronger.

Frances' motivation for writing the book.

Canadian writer Michael Francis McCarthy explained what was likely to have been in Frances's mind when she wrote *The Secret Garden*. She was, he said:

'devastated by the death of her eldest son, Lionel, from tuberculosis in 1890. To cope with her grief, she delved deeper into the "occult" after previously exploring the tenets of Spiritualism, Theosophy and [US religious leader] Mary Baker Eddy's Christian Science, amongst other late-nineteenth/early-twentieth-century millennial philosophies.' She 'rode the first wave of mind-body theory', and finally 'she began incorporating "New Thought" ideas into her writing and became one of its leading proponents'.

What is 'New Thought'? US psychologist and philosopher William James used this term as synonymous with the 'Mind Cure Movement'. In his book entitled *The Varieties of Religious Experience* (1902), James described 'the most characteristic feature of the Movement as follows:

'The leaders in this faith have had an intuitive belief in the all-saving power of healthy-minded attitudes as such, in the conquering efficacy of courage, hope, and trust, and a correlative contempt for doubt, fear, worry, and all nervously precautionary states of mind.'[4]

On 12 October 1913, in an interview with *The New York Times*, Frances declared:

'One thing is certain. The occult — the unknown (call it what you will) of to-day is the certain knowledge of to-morrow. We are on the eve of marvellous revelations. The air is surcharged with the thought of it. Ten years ago the word occult, to the masses, was a meaningless term; to-day it arouses intense interest. Think of it! The concentrated interest of millions of minds. What a vital force is there! What marvellous things may not this concentrated thought accomplish!'[5]

This, of course, is what Frances meant by her use of the word 'magic'.

McCarthy continued:

'We can therefore view *The Secret Garden* as a tribute to her dead son and as a wake-up call to the world about the "Beautiful Thought" (as she preferred to call the New Thought movement) — that people can heal themselves through positive thinking and affirmations, and that "all is one." After Lionel's death, it became part of her life's mission to spread the "Beautiful Thought" to the masses. *The Secret Garden* was her vehicle.'[6]

One may imagine Frances thinking to herself, 'The doctors failed to save my dear son Lionel but perhaps he could have been saved, had I known about and embraced the New Thought movement earlier. In any case, I hope my beliefs as set out in *The Secret Garden* will be a help and inspiration to others'.

Chapter 5

The Aforementioned 'Golden Age' Authors Compared

Of the seven 'Golden Age' authors described above, three featured characters that were purely human; one featured characters that were purely anthropomorphic; and three featured characters that were a mixture of both.

Of these seven authors, five used human-type settings for their stories; and two used settings that were surreal, i.e. Dodgson and his 'Wonderland' and Barrie and his 'Neverland'.

As regards motivation, Charles Dodgson, aka Lewis Carroll, was asked to write about Alice's Adventures in Wonderland by ten-year-old Alice Pleasance Liddell, in whose company he felt so relaxed that he temporarily lost his stammer, and he readily agreed. However, in doing so, by giving full vent to his wonderful wit and letting his vivid imagination run wild, Dodgson, would surely have derived much pleasure and personal satisfaction from the enterprise.

Edith Nesbitt's life was blighted by bereavement and poverty. However, by utilising her talents as a writer, she was able to keep herself and her family afloat. Not only that, she took the opportunity of using her book *The Railway Children* as a vehicle to disseminate her values to the wider world: the kindness which both family and strangers are capable of; and the virtues of thrift and dogged determination.

In *The Jungle Book,* Rudyard Kipling anthropomorphised the animals which he had encountered whilst living in India. However, it is essentially about a human child who is abandoned by his parents. The story parallels Kipling's own life, when he too felt abandoned having been sent as a child from India to live with strangers in the UK. In a sense, *The Jungle Book* is therefore a cry for help on Kipling's part.

Kenneth Grahame anthropomorphised the animals that he had encountered as a child on the riverbank to create stories with which he entertained his son. These stories were the origin of *The Wind in the Willows*. The book extolled the values of empathy, friendship, loyalty, and the importance of the home, values which Grahame undoubtedly endorsed.

Beatrix Potter, in *The Tale of Peter Rabbit* and in other 'Tales', anthropomorphised the animals that she had owned as pets as a child, and also those that she had encountered as an adult in the Lake District to create stories that were intended to bring comfort to a poorly child of her acquaintance.

Frances Hodgson Burnett's *The Railway Children* featured a little girl who became an orphan, yet by her strength of character, she still had the capacity to be strong and supportive to others. The story therefore gives a message of hope: that if you think positively and take life by the proverbial scruff of the neck, you will overcome your difficulties and succeed.

J. M. Barrie, in *Peter Pan*, created the story of a little boy who is abandoned by his mother, but who finds a substitute mother to love him. This echoes Barrie's own personal feelings of rejection by his own mother and is in a sense a cry of anguish from the author.

What is striking about the aforementioned authors is that none of their writings for children came out of nothing. There was a catalyst in every case, and they were inspired for various reasons, including a sense of altruism (a disinterested and selfless concern for the well-being of others[1]); a desire to help others in distress; or as a result of the authors' own personal anguish and heartache.

The lives of A. A. Milne, creator of *Winnie-the-Pooh* and *The House at Pooh Corner*, who also rightly appears in the pantheon of 'Golden Age' authors, and of his illustrator E. H. Shepard, will now be examined.

Chapter 6

A. A. Milne (born 18 January 1882)

Alan Alexander Milne was born in Hampstead on 18 January 1882. He attended Henley House School, where his father was headmaster and one of his teachers was novelist H. G. Wells. He subsequently attended Westminster (public i.e., independent, fee-paying) School.

Milne described his cricketing days at Westminster School, which he attended with his older brother Ken. 'Age and influence' would lead a budding young cricketer like himself to a 'house net' [i.e., a trial in the practice area], and 'skill' to a school net.

'Because, I must suppose, I was so small and looked so young (and promising), because I ran about so actively at football and played so enthusiastically down the long corridor on Saturday evenings, there was a Milne chosen for the net and it was I, not Ken.'

The outcome was that 'In my last year I got my pinks or School colours'. Nonetheless, said Milne modestly, 'At cricket Ken was definitely the better of the two; we both had enthusiasm, but he had style'. As for Ken, in his final year 'he did get his 3rd XI colours'.

It was through cricket, and in particular through a fellow member of the Allahakbarries Cricket Club - about which more will be said shortly - that Milne was put in touch with E. H. Shepard and as the result of a joint venture, they would become household names.

From Westminster School, Milne won a scholarship to Trinity College, Cambridge. He graduated in 1903 with a B.A. in Mathematics. While at university, Milne also edited the student magazine Granta.

After leaving university he worked as a freelance writer until being appointed assistant editor of *Punch* magazine in 1906 at the age of 24. *Punch* magazine of Fleet Street, London, was a humorous and satirical weekly established in 1841 by journalist, playwright and reformer Henry Mayhew, and wood-engraver Ebenezer Landells.

Chapter 7

Cricket

The life of a writer can be a solitary one, but it was through the game of cricket that Milne made some valuable contacts who would serve to further his literary career, though not altogether in the way that he had Planned! Cricket, as will be seen, was one of Milne's great passions!

In 1887 the Allahakbarries Cricket Club was founded by Scottish novelist and playwright James Matthew ('J. M.') Barrie. In October 1910, Milne:

'was invited by Barrie to become the last member of the Allahakbarries, the team having not played for the previous five years. The introduction came about because of their mutual friend, Edward Verrall ('E. V.') Lucas',[1] a journalist, poet, novelist and playwright with an extraordinarily wide range of interests. He was a former member of J. M. Barrie's Allahakbarries cricket team and, from 1908 to 1924, a reader for the London publishing house Methuen & Co. (founded in 1889 by Sir Algernon Methuen) and its chairman from 1924.

Membership of the club not only provided the opportunity for a convivial game of cricket, but it also gave its like-minded literati the chance to exchange ideas, and to 'network' – to interact with others and develop professional or social contacts.[2] And all this under the leadership of the immensely witty and sociable J. M. Barrie!

As for Lucas, one day he would introduce Milne to an illustrator, who would have a transformative effect on a number of Milne's books.

J. M. Barrie was born on 9 May 1860 in Kirriemuir, Angus, Scotland. His father, David, was a weaver, married to Margaret (née Ogilvy). Barrie attended three academies in succession, namely Glasgow, Forfar, and Dumfries.

'It was growing up in Kirriemuir that Barrie first learnt to play cricket, as he remarks in a letter from 1899 to an opposition captain whom he was arranging to meet in his home town.' As for the cricket pitch in Kirriemuir, this occupied 'a wild and windswept position just above the cemetery at the top of Kirrie Hill'.[3] It was during his attendance at Dumfries Academy that he was noted as 'having some success at left-arm bowling for his school'.[4]

On 21 April 1882 Barrie graduated from Edinburgh University with an M.A. in Literature. He first became a journalist and subsequently a novelist and playwright. In March 1885, Barrie relocated to London. On 9 July 1894, he married actress Mary Ansell.

On 27 December 1904, Barrie's most famous work, the play *Peter Pan*, or *The Boy Who Wouldn't Grow Up*, had its first stage performance at the Duke of York's Theatre in London's West End. In 1928, his novel, *Peter Pan and Wendy*, was published by Hodder & Stoughton.

Former Allahakbarries who had previously been associated with *Punch* magazine were cartoonist Edward Tennyson Reed; author of children's stories Charles Turley Smith; illustrator Richard Doyle, uncle of Arthur Conan Doyle; and actor Gerald du Maurier, son of George du Maurier (*Punch*'s social cartoonist from 1864 until his death in 1896).

What of the Allahakbarries? It was during the course of 'long tramps in Surrey', said Barrie, 'oftenmost to lovely Shere', a village near Guildford, in the company of Gilmour and Australian-born British novelist, journalist, playwright, and short-story writer Marriott Watson, that:

'they talked so much cricket that it began to be felt among them that they were hidden adepts at the game, and an ambition came over them to unveil. This was strengthened by the elderly appearance of the Shere [cricket] team, whom they decided to challenge after letting them grow one year older. Anon [i.e., Barrie] was appointed captain (by chicanery it is said by the survivors), and he thought there would be no difficulty in getting a stout XI, together, literary men being such authorities on the willow.'

'On the eventful day', said Barrie, with the sense of humour for which he was renowned:

'he found out in the railway compartment by which they advanced upon Shere that he had to coach more than one of his players in the finesse of the game: which was the side of the bat you hit with, for instance. In so far as was feasible they also practised in the train.'

How did the club get its name? Barrie explained. 'Two of the team were African travellers of renown, Paul du Chaillu [French-US zoologist] of gorilla fame and the much-loved Joseph Thomson [African explorer] of Masailand.' When Barrie enquired of them 'What was the African [i.e. Arabic]' for 'Heaven help us', they replied, 'Allahakbar':

'So, they decided to call themselves the Allahakbars, afterwards changed with complimentary intention to the Allahakbarries' – 'barries' being a compliment to Barrie, the club's founder.

In fact, the Arabic for 'Heaven help us' is 'Aljanat sawf tusaeiduna', 'Allah' being the Arabic word for 'God'.

The team 'played a few matches yearly for several summers, that first one being the most ignominious' when 'On the glorious hill-top of Albury [a village near Guildford] … they were overwhelmed that day by Shere'!

How had Barrie, a Scotsman, first become interested in cricket? Calling himself 'Anon', he declared:

'Cricket had been my joy since I first saw it played in infancy by valiant performers in my native parts, and Anon was not long in London before he found his way to Lord's [cricket ground in St John's Wood, London, known as the 'Home of Cricket']. The most charming sight he saw there was at an Eton and Harrow match'[5] played between two of England's leading public schools.

On 28 July 1913, the Allahakbarries played what was to be their final game, at Downe House School, Downe, in Kent against an XI captained by E. V. Lucas. The school, where Lucas's daughter Audrey was then a boarder, had been founded in 1907, the house having once been the home of

Charles Darwin, naturalist and co-propounder with Alfred Russel Wallace of the Theory of Evolution.

A photograph of some of the members of those two teams features not only Lucas, but Milne himself. Other members include George Llewelyn Davies (aged 19, who inspired the character of Peter Pan); Thomas Lennox Gilmour, barrister, journalist, and author; William Maxse Meredith, publisher and bookseller, and George Meredith junior, who were both sons of the novelist George Meredith; Denis Mackail, novelist, short story writer, and author of the official biography of J. M. Barrie; Harry Graham, soldier, writer, journalist, and lyricist; Dr Ernest Goffe, physician; Maurice Hewlett, lawyer, historical novelist, poet and essayist; J. M. Barrie himself; George Morrow, cartoonist and book illustrator; Walter Frith, barrister, author, and drama critic; Percy Lucas, brother of E. V. Lucas, Director of the School of Morris Dancing, Chelsea; T. Wrigley (not identified), Charles Tennyson, grandson and biographer of the poet Alfred Tennyson; and William ('Willie') Winter, nephew of J. M. Barrie and author of books on chess. Audrey Lucas, daughter of E. V. Lucas, also appeared in the photograph.

Arthur Conan Doyle, writer, doctor, and creator of the fictional detective Sherlock Holmes was a member of the XI at that time.

Although Milne played only one game for the Allahakbarries, being in the presence of so many literati would have been a great joy to him. As for Barrie, his humour and self-deprecatory wit endeared him to them all. For example, in his booklet *Allahakbarries C. C.* [Cricket Club] *1893*, Barrie described himself as:

'An incomparable Captain. The life and soul of his side. A treat to see him tossing the penny. Hits well off his pads. Once took a wicket.'

And in an eponymously named booklet, published in 1899, Barrie included the following 'Hints: To the Team by their Captain':

1 'I don't practise on opponents' ground before match begins. This can only give them confidence.
2 Each man, when he goes in, to tap the ground with his bat.
3 Should you hit the ball, run at once. Don't stop to cheer.
4 No batsman is allowed to choose his own bowler. You needn't think it.

5 Partridge [J. Bernard, illustrator], when bowing, keep your eye on square-leg.
6 Square-leg, when Partridge is bowling. Keep your eye on him.
7 If bowled first ball, pretend that you only came out for the fun of the thing, and then go away and sit by yourself behind the hedge.[6]

Anyone familiar with cricket and its rules and etiquette, as indeed Milne was, would have found these remarks to be utterly hilarious!

Apart from their literary associations, what several of the members of the 1913 Allahakbarries Cricket XI had in common was their association with *Punch* magazine. For example, E. V. Lucas joined the staff of *Punch* in 1904 as deputy editor and remained with the magazine for more than thirty years. George Morrow joined the magazine in 1906 and contributed cartoons to it. Harry Graham also contributed to *Punch*, as did Milne himself for whom it was a springboard to greater successes.

Another Allahakbarrie was Owen Seaman, who 'had been a contributor to *Punch* since 1894 and had been invited to join the famous table in 1897'.[7] Seaman became the assistant editor of *Punch* in 1902 and editor from 1906 to 1932. After making the score of '2 not out' in the so-called 'Test Match' of 1898, Seaman composed a poem entitled 'The Winning Hit':

> Bloody the battle, and the sun was hot,
> When on our ranks there fell an awful rot.
> One bearded warrior, playing like a Blue,
> Had made a prehistoric swipe for two,
> When three, his fellows, noted for their pluck,
> Through inadvertence got a paltry duck.[8]

'Blue': a person who has represented Oxford or Cambridge University in a particular sport – in this case cricket. 'Duck': a batsman's score of nought.[9]

In 1904, when Sir Francis C. Burnand, who had been editor of *Punch* from 1880 to 1906 retired, he was succeeded by Seaman. Whereupon one of Seaman's first actions was to appoint Milne as his assistant editor. This was, 'despite the fact that the two men did not get along at all'.[10] Furthermore, Milne described Seaman as 'a strange, unlucky man'.[11]

One may imagine the joy that the Allahakbarries had in their cricket, in those days long before the advent of professionalism, when it was not necessary to cover oneself in protective clothing in anticipation of a cricket ball arriving at speeds of almost 100 mph; or to wear a protective helmet and visor; or to make sure that there was a cardiac defibrillator to hand for emergencies! This was a leisurely game, albeit competitive, played in the peaceful settings of rural England and Scotland by men, and by women also, for pure enjoyment rather than for fame or any pecuniary reward.

Milne was also a member of the Authors' Cricket Club, founded in 1892, which played up until 1912. Here, he would have come into contact with other notable literati, such as the aforementioned Arthur Conan Doyle and author and humourist P. G. Wodehouse. Lucas and Barrie were also members.

If members of the Allahakbarries and the Authors' XI, past and present, were to be added together, the list would read like a 'Who's Who' of the UK's literary establishment. Furthermore, it was Milne's association with the two cricket clubs, and also with *Punch* magazine, that brought him an introduction to the illustrator E. H. Shepard, who, when Milne came to write his four legendary *Winnie-the-Pooh* books, would elevate them to an even more glorious dimension! The circumstances in which this great collaboration came about will be discussed shortly.

Chapter 8

A. A. Milne and *Punch* Magazine

The road along which Milne travelled to achieve success with *Punch* magazine had been long and hard, but he was ultimately successful, up to a point.

Having left university and become a freelance writer, Milne stated that '*Punch* remained my goal, and I was no nearer to it. Every week I sent something in, and every week it came back again.'[1] But he kept trying, nevertheless. 'There was a legend in those days that the contributor of any joke to *Punch*, illustrated or not, received £5 for it.' In April 1904:

'I made my first contribution to the paper, a four-line paragraph. I might get £5 and, if so, I was a made man; but was it possible on the strength of one paragraph, to say that I wrote for *Punch*? Hardly. However, I had little time in which to wonder.'

'In the following week the miracle happened, and a set of verses forced itself past Seaman into the paper. I was a real *Punch* contributor at last. To consolidate my position still more thoroughly, I had a small prose contribution, a narrow column, in the next number. All was well. I had proved that I could earn a living by writing. I would be Editor of *Punch* one day. I was the happiest man in London.'[2]

Sadly, however, Milne considered that the remuneration that he had received for 'my three April contributions' was insufficient. 'There was no object now in sending contributions to *Punch*.' He therefore 'renounced' his aspirations to the editorship.[3]

Subsequently, said Milne, he composed 'A very funny dialogue' about 'those famous wrestlers', Georg Hackenschmidt, an Estonian, and Ahmed

Madrali, a Turk. This was rejected by various publishers, but '*Punch* printed it', and '*Punch* sent me a cheque for £5. All was well again'.[4]

Having become a regular contributor to *Punch,* Milne, as already mentioned, was appointed its assistant editor in 1906 at the age of only 24.

In 1910, he was finally granted a seat at the *Punch* table, on the surface of which he duly carved his initials 'A. A. M.' in the traditional way. And in that same year, he said, 'I published what I think of now as my first book: *The Day's Play*, a collection of *Punch* articles'.[5]

On 4 June 1913, Milne married Dorothy de Sélincourt ('Daphne to friends'), who was Seaman's god-daughter. Daphne's father Martin was a cloth and silk merchant of Paddington, London, married to Mabel (née Speed). The newlyweds:

'Took a flat in Embankment Gardens, Chelsea. I was now getting eight guineas a week for my contributions to *Punch*, which was then the top price for writers on the staff.'[6]

Chapter 9

The First World War (1914-1918): Milne Enlists

The First World War broke out on 24 July 1914. It was fought between the Allies (French, Russian, British, Japanese, and Italian) and the Central Powers (Germany, Austria-Hungary, the Ottoman Empire and Bulgaria). The USA did not join the Allies and declare war on Germany until 6 April 1917. For the Allies, military casualties totalled an estimated 7½ million, compared to 5½ million for the Central Powers.

It was 'as the result of an introduction' from the poet Robert Graves' said Milne, that he was commissioned to the 4th Battalion of the 11th Royal Warwickshire Regiment:

'then stationed at Golden Hill in the Isle Wight. After six experimental weeks in which I learnt to be just a little, but not much, like a soldier, Daphne joined the married strength, and from then on, whenever it was possible, she shared the war with me. Through a variety of accidents, I became Signalling Officer.'[1] In fact, in the four years of the First World War, said Milne, he rose 'like a rocket from Second Lieutenant to Full Lieutenant.[2] The question is, would Milne, who had enlisted in the British Army, survive the war unscathed?

'When war broke out in 1914, there were less than 6,000 men in the Royal Engineers Signal Service, 3,000 of whom were partially trained signal units of the Territorial Force. By the end of the war there were 70,000 signallers.'[3]

'After a nine weeks' course at the Southern Command Signalling School', said Milne, 'I really knew something about it, with the result that I was kept at home as an instructor until July 1916.'[4] During this time, he said, his wife

Daphne, wrote, to his dictation, 'a little play about a Prince and Princess, and a Wicked Countess [after which Milne mischievously wrote 'Daphne' in brackets!], and a magic ring'.

Having returned from his signalling course, Milne continued, he 'rejoined the battalion which had now moved to Sandown, and we had taken the prettiest cottage in the town with lilacs and cherry-trees in the garden'. He now dictated another book, this time 'a long fairy-story called *Once on a Time*'.[5] Milne's creative spirit therefore continued to burn brightly, despite the circumstances at the time.

Chapter 10

Types of Signalling Equipment

'At the start of the First World War, flags were also used for signalling, but this practice was little used as the war years progressed.'[1]

'In August 1914, the Signal Service relied largely on the telegraph [a system for transmitting messages from a distance along a wire, especially one creating signals by making and breaking electrical connections[2]], visual communications, liaison officers and runners [messengers], including motorcycle despatch riders ("DonRs" - Don being "D" in the WW1 phonetic alphabet). During the initial highly mobile action, there wasn't time to set up complex telegraph networks, so there was great reliance on runners.'[3]

'Where it was not possible to lay landlines then many forms of visual signalling were used which made use of light either from sunlight (use of the sun and mirrors) in daytime and lamps at night (Lucas Lamps).'

The 'Lucas Lamp' was invented by Oliver Lucas of the Birmingham lamp-making company Joseph Lucas & Son (founded in 1897) in 1916. 'Messages were sent in Morse code, one man operating the signalling device and one man using a telescope (where distances were great) to read the message sent back.'

'The standard field telephone used with landlines consisted of a wooden box containing two dry cells, a magneto generator, polarised bell, induction coil testing plug, and a "Hand Telephone C Mk.1." Towards the end of 1916 these were replaced by the Fullerphone and by 1918 many Divisions adopted them in their forward positions.'[4]

The Fullerphone, with which Milne would have been familiar, was invented in 1915 by Captain Algernon Fuller of the Royal Engineers Signal Service.

'The signal was sent in Morse using a very small DC, filtered to eliminate the sharp, and detectable, voltage changes that accompanied current transitions when keying. At the receiving end the DC was converted to AC by a continuously running mechanical "chopper" and listened to through a sensitive earpiece.'

This invention made it virtually impossible for the enemy to intercept the signals through the earth.[5]

Another device with which Milne would have been familiar was the heliograph, by which sunlight is reflected in flashes from a mobile mirror.[6] Such devices were:

'used for signalling to a distant point. It comprised of a wooden tripod of which each leg was adjustable. The mirror assembly for this device was usually kept safely packed in a stout leather or wooden box.'[7]
'In 1915 the French gave the British 15 pigeons' and these 'carrier pigeons' soon became 'a valuable supplementary method of communication. By the end of the war the British Army had more than 20,000 pigeons.'[8]

'Animals carried equipment and helped to lay line [cable]. Dogs proved particularly adaptable and were trained to lay line and carry messages'. A photograph exists of such an animal, walking along as the line pays out from a reel strapped to its back.[9]

Finally, if large amounts of cable were required to be laid over long distances, a 'Cable Wagon' was employed:

'pulled by 6 horses and accompanied by a team of outriders. These wagons were modifications of an artillery gun carriage. They were used extensively to lay cable during mobile phases of the war.'[10]

Chapter 11

The Task of the Signaller

The Royal Engineers Signal Service was created in 1912:

'and made responsible for telegraph, telephone, signal despatch and, later, wireless communications from General Headquarters (GHQ) down to brigades and for artillery communications down to batteries. Regimental signallers were responsible for communications within their own units and from units to brigades.'[1]

The huge extent to which the army depended on signalling is illustrated by the following statement:

'After the initial mobile phase in France the armies faced each other for 3½ years across 500 miles of trenches. "Line" (telegraph and telephone) was the most common means of communication. Line in forward areas was insulated and laid on or below ground. It was known as "cable" and was vulnerable to artillery fire. To protect cables within enemy artillery range they needed to be armoured, buried to a depth of at least 6 ft and camouflaged. To prevent spotting from the air, the burying was carried out at night.'

'Initially, to save cable, a single-cable earth return system was used for telegraph. These circuits just used one wire. The second wire, or return path, was replaced by using a ground spike, stuck in the earth. This used the earth's conductivity to complete the circuit.'

The duties of a signaller, the methods used, and just how dangerous this occupation was are illustrated by the following article:

'During the First World War, being a signaller usually meant you were close to the front-line troops, providing signals communications back to your Company and Battalion HQ. Wired telephones were used where possible, but this involved laying landlines which was a hazardous job due to enemy shelling.'

'Signallers were also used in forward positions to assist the artillery and provide information on their enemy targets. In these positions, often isolated, the signaller became vulnerable to enemy shelling and attack, and many signallers lost their lives.'[2] Milne witnessed this at close hand, as will be seen.

Chapter 12

Milne Goes Into Action

The Battle of the Somme (1 July to 18 November 1916), in which Milne participated, was an offensive conducted by the Allies against the Central Powers and fought on either side of the eponymous northern French river. 'Before and during the battle, over 50,000 miles of cable were laid, of which 7,000 miles in the forward areas were buried.'[1]

'I was attached to the 11th Battalion of the [Royal Warwickshire] regiment, then commanded by Lieut. Colonel C. S. Collison.'[2] 2. However, 'I had been sent, with the military efficiency of those days', said Milne dryly, 'to a battalion which had already a signalling officer, a new man just appointed, called Harrison.' This was Senior Signalling Officer Kenneth Harrison. 'I had spent eighteen months learning to be a signaller, and of bombs and rifles and the ordinary routine of the platoon officer I had forgotten what little I had known'.

'The brigade was just going into action. It proposed to capture the Switch Line [connecting two lines of trenches] at Bazentin-le-Petit [Somme department], or what once was that village. When this business was over, the Colonel would recommend my transference to some battalion which wanted those eighteen months' training; meanwhile I could go into action with the signalling officer and add some practical knowledge to all the theory which I had assimilated.'[3]

'As soon as we had got into the reserve trenches' said Milne:

'I went into the signallers' dugout to introduce myself; I liked signallers and felt at home with them. I meant to have asked a thousand technical questions but found myself engaged in a long discussion with Lance

Corporal Grainger about books. He was a Welsh miner, as well educated as most of them are, quiet, friendly, charming. We found that we shared a passion for Jane Austen.'[4] English literature was never far from Milne's mind, but the harsh reality of war soon became apparent.

On 8 August 1916, Milne's best friend, 2nd Lieutenant Ernest J. Pusch of the 11th Royal Warwickshire Regiment, son of Russian-born parents, was killed, aged 19, by an exploding shell. Six weeks earlier, the late Ernest's brother Frederick L. Pusch of the Irish Guards had also been killed, aged 20, by an enemy sniper. Meanwhile, Milne continued:

The attack commenced at midnight on 24 July 1916 and it was successful.

'On the day before, Harrison and three men, with me hanging on "for training", ran out a line to the front trench by a devious route, for we had been told that the existing line would never stand against the opening counter-barrage. On the way we fell into a burst of whizz-bangs [light shells fired from small calibre field guns], and Harrison was knocked out. We got him back to the first-aid post, I reported to the Colonel, and became signalling officer.'

'At four o'clock next morning we went out again, this time by the ordinary communication trench, such as it was, and laid a line, elaborately laddered according to the textbooks, and guaranteed to withstand any bombardment.'[5]

'Laddering is explained thus. The front line was linked by two lines:

'laid from front to rear with an interval of the order of 60 yards between them. These were then cross-connected by a number of lateral lines, the resulting network resembling the uprights and rungs of a ladder. Such a device minimized the likelihood of a complete disconnection, although individual breaks were more difficult to locate. Laddered cable was very useful during and immediately after an advance or a retreat and became at one time very generally used. The main drawback to its use was the necessity for constant overhaul of the whole network in order to ensure efficiency. If this was not done systematically, weak places would accumulate, until a final break might render the line useless.'[6]

'In an adjoining dug-out was the HQ of the East Lancashires with whom the attack was being made. The sergeant-major of the East Lancashires went up the steps with some idea, I suppose, of getting information, and was blown out of existence before he reached the top. My signallers announced this, and added that the line to Brigade was also down. We sat there completely isolated.'[7]

'It was about two o'clock in the morning that a runner got through. The attack, as was to be expected, was a complete failure. In his Company, So-and-so and So-and-so were killed. I remembered them, two boys under the apple trees in the little village where I had joined them in billets; we had dined in the garden to the gramophone, and there were peaches which one of them had fetched from Amiens, and the war was just a happy picnic to them, the guns rolling so far, far away in the distance ....'[8]

'I told my sergeant that we were now going to run out a line and asked him to pick two men for me. I knew nothing of the section then, save that there was a lance corporal [the aforementioned Grainger] who loved Jane Austen, unhelpful knowledge in the circumstances. He said at once: "I'll come, for one, sir", which I thought was sporting of him, although it was obviously wrong for both of us to go. He picked on another man, a company signaller who had joined headquarters for the occasion, and we attached ourselves to the Major. We dashed. The Major went first - he was going to "reorganize the troops"; I went second, God knew why; the sergeant and the signaller came behind me, running out a line neatly and skilfully. No laddering now, no textbook stuff, it was just dropped anywhere.'

'From time to time the Major flung himself down for a breather, and down we flopped and panted, wondering if he would get up again. To our relief each time he was alive, and so were we.'

'We passed one of the signal stations, no longer a station but a pancake of earth on top of a spreadeagled body; I had left him there that evening, saying, "Well, you'll be comfortable here". More rushes [sudden attacks, or onslaughts], more breathers, more bodies, we were in the front line.' We put in a week at Loos after the Somme.'[9] Loos was a quieter theatre of war.

As signallers, Milne and his men were clearly in great danger and in daily contact with violent death. But there were other hazards, as he was now to discover.

'I had my men out on a little hill one morning, and was walking as usual from station to station to see how the messages were coming through. It was a warm November day, so warm that each station seemed a mile, rather than a few hundred yards, from the next, and I wondered how I could drag my legs there.'

'At lunch in the HQ mess I went to sleep; spent the afternoon and evening sleeping in front of the stove; and when I went to bed I was given the usual couple of aspirins by the M.O. Next morning my temperature was 103. The M.O. went off to arrange for an ambulance to take me to the [casualty] clearing station. By the time I was introduced to it again, the thermometer was soaring up to 105. Next day the battalion got the order to move; the attack was to begin.'

Milne was suffering from trench fever, a disease caused by the bacteria *Bartonella quintana* and carried by body lice. Its symptoms include fever, severe headache, and aching legs and back. It may last for several weeks, and relapses are common.

'My sergeant came to say goodbye to me. I handed over my maps, commended the section to his care, wished him luck, and went to sleep again. He was lucky. He only lost a leg.'

'Ten days later I was at Southampton. Some kind woman offered to write a telegram for me. It was to Daphne, saying that she would find me in hospital at Oxford. I woke up one afternoon and saw her at the end of the bed, crying.'[10]

In January 1917, Milne rejoined his regiment at Sandown and rented a cottage there. He now wrote his first play, *The Two Wishes*. It was a playwright, above all, that he aspired to be.

18 January 1917 'was my birthday', said Milne:

'In addition to letters from the family, there was one from J. M. Barrie. He wrote to say that [US actor and stage director Dion L.] Boucicault was putting on two one-act plays of his in a Triple Bill, and that if I could turn *Wurzel-Flummery* [a far-fetched comedy, which premiered in London in April 1917] into a two-act play, it might be used to complete the programme. One could hardly imagine a more exciting birthday present.'[11]

Meanwhile, said Milne, 'Our battalion was a unit of the Portsmouth Garrison, and had, like other battalions in the garrison, its own signal section. It was now decided to establish a signalling school at Fort Southwick [overlooking Portsmouth's naval base] at which all signallers of the garrison could be trained together. The school was divided into four companies, of one of which I was to be in charge.'[12] In April 1917 Milne was duly transferred to the Royal Signal Corps at Fort Southwick as Signals Instructor.

But Milne had not fully recovered from trench fever and, he said, Daphne:

'begged me to see the M.O. at the Fort. I saw him, he sent me down to the Military Hospital at Cosham [Portsmouth], I was kept there for a night, thumped all over in the morning, and passed on to the Convalescent Hospital at Osborne for three weeks.'[13]

The 'hospital' was a requisitioned wing of Osborne House, on the Isle of Wight, formerly the royal residence of Queen Victoria, which was donated to the state by her son King Edward VII in 1902. During the First World War, it served as a convalescent home for wounded officers. Despite all, Milne's creative instinct was still strong, and during his convalescence, he wrote another play, *Belinda* (which was staged by Boucicault in April 1918).[14] Meanwhile:

In mid-1917 a Medical Board recommended that Milne was only fit for sedentary work. He returned briefly to Fort Southwick but, in November 1917, he was recruited by the War Office [Department of the British Government responsible for the administration of the British Army]'s Military Intelligence Unit MI7, a secret propaganda unit.

He was discharged from the Army in February 191

Chapter 13

MI7b: *The Green Book*

In Milne's own words, 'I was now in the War Office, wore the green tabs of Intelligence and wrote (horrible word) [Milne's brackets] propaganda'. On account of his illness, he said:

'I had been marked for Home Service by a succession of medical boards, with the recommendation of sedentary work. If there is any work more sedentary than writing I do not know it; moreover, by a happy accident, it was the only work for which I was mentally fit. I had a room to myself and wrote pretty much what I liked. If it were not patriotic enough, or neglected to point the moral with sufficient hardihood, then the Major supplied the operative words in green pencil.'[1]

MI7b, the unit to which Milne was attached, was concerned with 'foreign and domestic propaganda, including press releases concerning army matters.' Said Intelligence historian Andrew Cook:

'the unit also kept an eye on the foreign press, countering negative stories and writing material intended for leaflets which would be dropped by hot air balloons.'[2]

Other departments of the Military Intelligence Section 7 (MI7), were:

MI7a – 'Censorship'.
MI7c – 'Translation and (from 1917) regulation of foreign visitors'.
MI7d – 'Foreign press propaganda and review (part of subsection (b) until subsection (d) was formed in late 1916'.

MI7b employed writers – i.e., authors who were adept in the use of language – 'to present a positive version of the war to those at home' and to create 'articles which showed a very negative view of the "Hun Corpse factories"'. However, in respect of the so-called Hun Corpse factories, it was subsequently admitted by UK Foreign Secretary Sir Austen Chamberlain, in 1925, that they did not actually exist. In a statement to the House of Commons, Chamberlain stated that there was "never any foundation" for what he called "this false report". In other words, it was a lie. In the same year, the Conservative MP John Charteris, who had served as Sir Douglas Haig's Chief Intelligence Officer at the British Expeditionary Force (BEF) Headquarters from 1915 to 1918, 'reportedly admitted, while on a lecture tour of the US, that he had fabricated the story.' The BEF comprised the six divisions that the British Army sent to the Western Front during the First World War.

Furthermore, in an article published in the *New York Times*, Charteris disclosed exactly how he had fabricated this false piece of British propaganda. He said that:

'he had transposed captions from one of two photographs found on captured German soldiers. One showed a train taking dead horses to be rendered, the other showed a train taking dead soldiers for burial.' According to British propaganda, soap and margarine were being extracted from these corpses![3] Not surprisingly, at the end of the war: 'the government ordered that all documents relating to the unit should be destroyed, because the work was highly secret. For almost 100 years it was thought that all MI7b documents had been lost forever. Then in August 2012, Jeremy Arter from Callow, near Hereford, was clearing his aunt's home in Talybont-on-Usk, near Brecon [South Wales], when he discovered some papers.

They were about to be thrown into a skip when Mr Arter spotted an official stamp on one of the documents - it was from MI7b.'

'On closer inspection Mr Arter found over 150 articles and papers written by his uncle, Capt. James Lloyd, and others who had worked with him in the propaganda unit MI7b.' Captain Lloyd of the Welsh Regiment was one of three brothers. He was wounded at Mametz Wood in 1916 and recruited by MI7b in 1917. Arter described how MI7b had been:

'"established to sustain support for the war at a crucial time when the numbers of soldiers killed were rising and social unrest threatened to undermine the military effort." The unit's stories were published by friendly newspaper proprietors and editors.'[4]

Rob Phillips, digitisation project manager at the National Library of Wales, which is currently creating an archive relating to the Welsh experience of the war, said: 'As far as we're aware this is the only surviving body of material from MI7b and it's a truly remarkable record of how the British propaganda machine worked at the time. Along with manuscripts and photographs, Arter found a pamphlet entitled *The Green Book*, dated January 1919 and stamped MI7b: "for private circulation".

Among the 20 or so of 'greatest literary men of their day who worked for MI7b', Arter mentioned crime writer Cecil Street; traveller and writer Roger Pocock; Irish poet Patrick MacGill; writer and satirist J. B. Morton; and, of course, A. A. Milne. As for *The Green Book*, Arter described it as:

'a valedictory [farewell] in-house magazine probably printed in no more than 20 copies', for each of the literati who had worked for MI7b. 'In it they vent their spleen and humour at the war and at each other. It's a priceless document. Great Uncle Jim [Captain John Lloyd] broke every rule in the book to preserve it.'[5]

Milne's contribution to *The Green Book* was to parody four famous poems: by Alfred Tennyson, Henry Wadsworth, William Shakespeare and Richard Lovelace respectively:

1. Lieut. Alfred Tennyson, of the Suffolks.
   'You must wake and call me early,
   call me early, Mother dear,
   While I tell how Tim and Curly
   went and pinched a pot of beer,
   And a blooming blinking sergeant
   was the one 'oo 'ad to pay –
   For that is the British way, Mother,
   that is the British way.'

2. Captain Thomas Campbell, of the Border Regiment.
   'It was the schooner *Hesperus*
   Which sailed the wintry seas

And victory *must* remain with us
While we have ships like these.'

3. Captain William Shakespeare, of a Cyclist Battalion.

'In M.I.7.B. [MI7b],
Who loves to lie with me
About atrocities
And Hun Corpse Factories
Come hither, come hither, come hither,
Here shall he see
No enemy,
But sit all day and blether.'

Milne's choice of this poem, which includes the word 'lie', which in the poem is taken to mean to assume a resting position, but which may also mean to make an intentionally false statement, implies that he was well aware that the story of the Hun Corpse Factories was a fiction!

4. Lieut. Lovelace, of the Royal Warwickshire Regt. (To his Colonel on coming from the War.)

'Tell me not, Sir, I am unkind
That from the Hunnery
Of Hindenburg's disgusting mind
To pen and ink I fly.
For this delection, so to speak,
Is one you must adore;
My "British Front from Week to Week"
Has helped to win the war!'

[signed] A. A. M.'[6]

Chapter 14

The War Ends

Anticipating the end of hostilities, which came with the signing of the Armistice on 11 November 1918, Milne declared:

'The war would be over any day now. What was I going to do? Duty (I thought) called me back to *Punch*; inclination to this new life in the theatre.' However, could he be sure of making a living 'as a dramatist':

'Wasn't I in a way pledged to *Punch*, which for the first three years of the war had paid me half my assistant-editor's salary? The answer to the first question was "No", to the second "Yes". I would go back to *Punch* for three years; then I should feel free. And by that time I hoped to have proved that I could live on the theatre.'

Milne, however, was doomed to disappointment. He hurried round to the *Punch* office and 'burst in' on Owen Seaman, who 'looked up, surprised. "Hallo?" he said. "I've come back", I announced dramatically.' The outcome was, said Milne, that Owen informed him that 'whatever happened, I should never be Editor' of the magazine.[1]

In *The Art of Winnie-the-Pooh*, published in 2017, its author James Campbell (husband of Shepard's great-granddaughter) suggested that Seaman's antipathy to Milne arose because he took the 'view that as a pacifist Milne was an unpatriotic radical, and he did not want a person with such views in a management position at the magazine'.[2] This, of course, is to ignore the fact that at the outbreak of the First World War, Milne had answered the call of Lord Kitchener, Secretary of State for War, and joined the British Army.

Despite this, when *The Sunny Side*, a collection of poems and essays by Milne was published in 1921, it included a dedication 'To Owen Seaman affectionately in memory of nine happy years at the "*Punch*" office'. Meanwhile, said Milne:

'Demobilization was not difficult. I rejoined the regiment at Crowborough [Sussex], where, as a sedentary soldier, I not only lived comfortably at the Beacon Hotel, but found a comfortable stool in the demobilization office from which I could call attention to the hard case of Lieut. A. A. Milne. In little more than a week I was in respectable [i.e., civilian] clothes again.'

Milne's three-act comedy play, *Mr Pim Passes By,* was 'finished and under consideration' by playwright and theatre producer John Drinkwater; his children's play, *Make Believe*, had coincided with actor and director Nigel Playfair's 'management of the Lyric, Hammersmith'; and 'in the summer' he had 'written a play called *The Great Broxopp* which was now being sent round' to various directors.[3] The latter play was about a son who feels that his life has been blighted by his father's success. This would one day have resonance in respect of the lives of Milne and his own son, Christopher. But for the present, what Milne really required was 'some sort of regular weekly income'.[4]

Milne became dramatic critic of *The Outlook* (a British weekly periodical established in 1889) for six weeks before he 'discovered that the position was impossible' because of potential conflicts of interest:

'One could not damn a manager's play and then send him a play of one's own; still less could one praise it and then send him a play of one's own.' And then with typical modesty, 'Least of all could one tell other dramatists how to write plays when one's own imperfect plays were available for comparison. So, I resigned'.[5]

'In the intervals I wrote a detective story. I had read most of those which had been written, admired their ingenuity, but didn't like their English. Their characters (in as far as they existed as characters, which was anaemically) continually "effected egresses", instead of "going out". The detective "carefully selected" a cigarette from his case (something which no human being has ever done) before telling his colleague what his impressions were when he first had "cognizance" of the affair.'

In other words, the language was too elaborate. 'I wondered if I could write a detective story about real people in real English.' The outcome was The *Red House Mystery*, which 'had a surprising success'.[6]

Now came an event which would alter the course of Milne's life, the birth of a son. On 21 August 1920, he said euphemistically, 'my collaborator produced a personal work'. But what name to give the infant child? He and his wife Daphne must decide.

'One of us thought of Robin, the other of Christopher.' But the names were 'wasted on him', said Milne, because his infant son 'called himself Billy Moon as soon as he could talk, and has been Moon to his family and friends ever since'.[7]

In his book *The Enchanted Places* (the name of the final story in his father's book *The House at Pooh Corner*, was 'An Enchanted Place'), published in 1974, Christopher himself explained how he had obtained his nickname:

'Moon, this was my early attempt at saying "Milne", superseded Billy within the family around 1925, and thereafter remained my father's only name for me; used by him among his friends and acquaintances on every occasion when something more precise than "my boy" was required. Universally used among close friends and family, my mother only excepted.'[8]

As for 'Billy', no explanation is offered for this.

The fact that everyone knew the child as 'Billy Moon', said Milne, 'explains why the publicity which came to be attached to Christopher Robin', publicity which was great indeed, as will shortly be seen, 'never seemed to affect us personally, but to concern either a character in a book or a horse which we hoped at one time would win the Derby'! In other words, to Milne, his son and his son's fictional namesake - who was soon to appear in the 'Pooh' storybooks - were two distinct and separate entities.

In 1923, when Christopher was aged 3, the Milne family relocated to North Wales.

The writing and illustrating of the Pooh books came about quite by chance. In 1923, writer and poet Rose Fyleman launched, and edited for two years, a children's magazine called *The Merry-Go-Round*. Whereupon, said Milne, 'She asked me, I have no idea why, to write some verses for it'. At first, he declined. 'I said that I didn't and couldn't, it wasn't in my line'. But then he changed his mind:

'I wrote to Miss Fyleman to say that perhaps after all I might write her some verses. A poem called 'The Dormouse and the Doctor' was the result. It was illustrated by [New Zealand-born British illustrator] Harry Rountree; proofs had come to me in Wales; and with them came letters from both illustrator and editor saying, "Why don't you write a whole book of verses like these?"'[9]

So Milne 'Took a pencil and an exercise book and escaped to the summer house' which 'contained a chair and a table'.[10]

'And there on the other side of the lawn was a child with whom I had lived for three years … and here within me were unforgettable memories of my own childhood … what was I writing? A child's book of verses obviously. Not a whole book, of course; but to write a few would be fun - until I was tired of it. Besides, my pencil had an india-rubber [eraser] at the back; just the thing for poetry.'

'I had eleven wet days in that summer house and wrote eleven sets of verses. Then we went back to London. By the end of the year, I had written enough for a book.'[11] It was entitled *When We Were Very Young*, and 'It was only after the book was in the publishers' hands that Owen Seaman heard about it. Probably Lucas, then chairman of Methuen, had mentioned it casually.'

'Owen asked if *Punch* could print some of it, and I told him, reluctantly enough, that he could use what he liked, for I feared that as a "reprint from *Punch*" it might not get the attention which would be given to a new book.'

'However, the publication of some of the verses had two good results; it confirmed my opinion that Shepard was the right illustrator for the book, and, with the first appearance of *The King's Breakfast*, gave the publishers an idea of its ultimate reception.' This was artist, book illustrator, and illustrator for *Punch*, Ernest Howard (E. H.) Shepard, who from 1921 was a regular staff cartoonist for the magazine.

The King's Breakfast was a whimsical story by A. A. Milne, its principal characters being the King, the Queen, a dairymaid and a cow! It was illustrated by E. H. Shepard and set to music by composer Harold Fraser-Simson.

This was the start of a collaboration between Shepard and Milne that was soon to make the two men famous throughout the world!

As for *The King's Breakfast*, said Milne, 'its ultimate reception … was enthusiastic beyond all imagining, both in England and America. In the ten years before it went into a cheap edition half a million copies were sold.'[12]

As for E. V. Lucas, said James Campbell, he:

'was so pleased by the impact of Shepard's illustrations in *Punch* that he commissioned him to illustrate his own forthcoming book of verse, *Playtime and Company*, and [author, educationist, and advocate of women's rights] Eva Erleigh's *The Little One's Log*.'[13]

Chapter 15

Milne and the First World War: Shell Shock

Milne was a pacifist who nevertheless played his part by joining the British Army and serving during the First World War. However, he subsequently remarked, 'It makes me almost physically sick of that nightmare of mental and moral degradation'.[1]

Although he survived the war without sustaining any serious physical injury, the question is, did Milne suffer mentally, having witnessed the scenes of horror as were visible on a daily basis on the Western Front?

A photograph exists of Milne, taken in 1922, just three years after the war had ended, when he was aged 40. In that photo, in which he is sitting with arms folded, Milne looks thin and gaunt, with a haunted look, dark shadows under his eyes, and pursed lips. He was a pipe smoker, and this is known to affect the complexion adversely, but perhaps not to so great a degree. The question therefore arises, was Milne still suffering from the adverse effects of the war?

Shell shock is defined as a psychological disturbance caused by prolonged exposure to active warfare, especially being under bombardment.[2] During the First World War 'doctors were mystified by a condition that they hadn't seen before. Soldiers were returning from the trenches blind, deaf, mute or paralysed'. To begin with, these symptoms were 'thought to be caused by soldiers being exposed to exploding shells'. However, 'Medical staff started to realise that there were deeper causes'. Doctors found, in many instances, 'that many men suffering the symptoms of shell shock without having even been in the front lines' and they 'couldn't find any physical damage to explain the symptoms'.

But not all army commanders were sympathetic to such men. During the course of the war, 'there were 240,000 Courts Martial and 3,080 death sentences handed down'. However:

'in only 346 cases was the sentence carried out. 266 British soldiers were executed for "Desertion", 18 for "Cowardice", 7 for "Quitting a post without authority", 5 for "Disobedience to a lawful command", and 2 for "Casting away arms".'[3]

It is likely that many of these accused men were suffering from the effects of stress and/or of exploding shells.

It was psychologist Charles S. Myers who first used the term 'shell shock' for the condition described above. In 1916 he was appointed consulting psychologist to the British Expeditionary Force. This was:

'In an effort to better understand and treat the condition, to offer opinions on cases of shell shock, and to gather data for a policy to address the burgeoning issue of psychiatric battle casualties. The War Office had turned him down for overseas service because of his age (he was 42), but undeterred, he crossed to France on his own initiative and secured a post at a hospital opened by the Duchess of Westminster in the casino at Le Touquet.'[4]

In February 1915, the following article by Myers was published in the weekly medical journal *The Lancet*: 'A Contribution to the Study of Shell Shock: Being an Account of Three Cases of Loss of Memory, Vision, Smell, and Taste, Admitted into the Duchess of Westminster's War Hospital, Le Touquet'.

Of the three shell-shocked men on whom Myers reported, all had experienced shells exploding in close proximity to them. He noted their symptoms as follows:

All three men experienced amblyopia (impaired or dim vision without obvious defect or change in the eye[5]); loss or absence of taste; distinct amnesia or slight loss of memory. One man experienced a slight loss of hearing.

Other symptoms were insomnia; 'woke up crying'; 'the slightest noise makes him start'; 'his hands became very tremulous and his forehead sweated profusely'; 'the slightest touch on his leg provoked well-marked spasm of the quadriceps muscle of the same thigh'.

The men were treated by hypnosis, with the aim of enabling them to recover the memory of the incident that had provoked the shell shock, in the hope that this memory would be retained once they emerged from hypnosis.[6] In reality, of course, it may have taken many explosions to produce shell shock in an individual.

'Myers argued that the military should set up specialist units "as remote from the sounds of warfare as is compatible with the preservation of the 'atmosphere' of the front". The army took his advice and allowed him to set up four specialist units in December 1916. They were designed to manage acute or mild cases, while chronic and severe cases were referred to base hospitals for more intensive therapy.'

'Myers proposed a system by which doctors would refer severe cases of shell shock directly from the base hospitals in France to specialist treatment centres in the United Kingdom. He argued that effective treatment required individual attention, which in turn demanded higher staffing ratios — ideally one doctor to 50 patients. To meet this demand, he persuaded the War Office to set up training courses in the principles and practice of military psychiatry and, in particular, the treatment of shell shock.'[7]

The huge number of shell shock cases was completely unexpected. By 1915 there was a shortage of hospital beds for sufferers. Many county lunatic asylums, private mental institutions, and disused spas were taken over and designated as hospitals for mental diseases and war neurosis. By 1918 there were over 20 such hospitals in the U.K. At the end of the war over 80,000 cases of shell shock had passed through British Army medical facilities.'[8]

Despite the vast resources allocated by the government to the treatment of shell shock, such treatment was only available to the most severely affected, and little thought would have been given to those such as Milne who displayed no obvious symptoms. But was this a possibility?

Certainly, there was no obvious sign of it, but of course for a former public schoolboy, a 'stiff upper lip' was the order of the day, and 'whingeing' would have been seen as a sign of weakness. However, it was in his writing and particularly in his poetry that Milne expressed his inner thoughts most deeply, for example, in his poem '*From a Full Heart*', first published in

Punch and then as part of a collection of poems and short stories published as *The Sunny Side* in 1921. (Author's comments in italics):

'In days of peace my fellow-men
Rightly regarded me as more like
A Bishop than a Major-Gen.,
And nothing since has made me warlike …'

Milne was originally a pacifist. The poem continues:

'But when this age-long struggle ends
And I have seen the Allies dish up
The goose of Hindenburg — oh, friends!
I shall out-bish the mildest Bishop.'

'When the War is over and the Kaiser's out of print,
I'm going to buy some tortoises and watch the beggars sprint;

When the War is over and the sword at last we sheathe,
I'm going to keep a jelly-fish and listen to it breathe.'

This implies that Milne longed for quietness, after the clamour of war.

'I never really longed for gore,
And any taste for red corpuscles
That lingered with me left before
The German troops had entered Brussels.
In early days the Colonel's "Shun!"
Froze me; and, as the War grew older,
The noise of someone else's gun
Left me considerably colder.'

'When the War is over and the battle has been won,
I'm going to buy a barnacle and take it for a run;
When the War is over and the German Fleet we sink,
I'm going to keep a silk-worm's egg and listen to it think.'

'The Captains and the Kings depart —
It may be so, but not lieutenants;
Dawn after weary dawn I start
The never-ending round of penance;
One rock amid the welter stands
On which my gaze is fixed intently —
An after-life in quiet hands
Lived very lazily and gently.'

Milne longs for rest and relaxation.

'When the War is over and we've done the Belgians proud,
I'm going to keep a chrysalis and read to it aloud;
When the War is over and we've finished up the show,
I'm going to plant a lemon-pip and listen to it grow.'

'Oh, I'm tired of the noise and the turmoil of battle
And I'm even upset by the lowing of cattle, And the clang of the bluebells is death to my liver,
And the roar of the dandelion gives me a shiver,
And a glacier, in movement, is much too exciting,
And I'm nervous, when standing on one, of alighting—
Give me Peace; that is all, that is all that I seek…
Say, starting on Saturday week.'[9]

The slightest noise or disturbance distresses Milne, who longs for peace.

Milne's poem '*From a Full Heart*' was therefore written by a person who had experienced and was continuing to experience shell shock.

In another paper, this time published in *The Lancet* in January 1916, Myers declared in respect of one of his patients, that it was only after a second hypnosis that he showed real progress:

'When he awoke from hypnosis the suggestion which I gave him before waking that he would remember all that he had told me proved only imperfectly effective. He could not remember his name, regiment, number, nor the names of his native village and the neighbouring town'. However, 'When he was re-hypnotized without delay, his memory became much clearer and ampler than before, and he was far more certain of his past history.'

In respect of another patient, said Myers: 'Under hypnosis he was able to recall all the events during the period of his previous amnesia. He remembered the direction from which the shell came, how he was lifted up, how be fell on his back, etc. As he passed into a deeper state of hypnosis the contractions of the sartorius [thigh muscle] muscles became very much diminished but did not absolutely disappear.' On being roused from hypnosis, said Myers, the involuntary movements 'at once ceased, and he awoke able to stand, absolutely free from his headache and spasmodic movements, with recovery of memory and, as other observers spontaneously remarked, "looking another man".'

'Indeed, in all these cases, whenever the memories dissociated from the normal personality were revived, they were accompanied by an outburst of emotion, sometimes of frenzy, but generally of fear. But in the cases described in this communication it was impossible without the help of hypnosis to obtain any revival of the lost memory.'

'After nine months of special work in France and Belgium upon these disorders, I have not the slightest hesitation in maintaining the genuineness of the cases above described.'

Myers summarized the results of his hypnotic treatment of shell-shocked patients as follows:

'At the time of writing I have hypnotized, or attempted to hypnotize, 23 cases of shell shock. The conditions under which I worked were such that no patient was subjected to further hypnotic treatment unless he proved readily hypnotizable on the first trial. The immediate results may be summarized:

(1) Apparently complete cures	26 per cent.
(2) Distinct improvement	26 "
(3) Failure to hypnotize	35 "
(4) No improvement after hypnosis	13 "

'It may be argued that mutism, rhythmical spasms, anaesthesia, and similar purely "functional" disturbances disappear after a time without specific treatment. But no one who has witnessed the unfeigned delight with which these patients, on waking from hypnosis, hail their recovery from such disorders can have any hesitation as to the impetus thus given towards a final cure. More especially is this the case in regard to the restoration of lost memories. Enough has been already said here about the striking changes in temperament, thought, and behaviour which follow on recovery from the amnesia.'

Myers did admit, however, that 'recoveries after hypnosis may not be immediately complete or permanent'.[10]

Today, shell shock, now known as Post-Traumatic Stress Disorder (PTSD), is treated by counselling and Cognitive Behavioural Therapy (CBT):

'CBT focuses on challenging and changing cognitive distortions (e.g., thoughts, beliefs, and attitudes) and behaviours, improving emotional regulation, and the development of personal coping strategies that target solving current problems.'[11] However, many believe that there is still a place for hypnosis in the treatment of PTSD. Sadly, no such help was available to A. A. Milne and countless others, during and after the First World War.

Chapter 16

Christopher Robin Milne (born 21 August 1920)

The relationship between Alan Milne and his son Christopher was of crucial importance in respect of four books of poetry and prose which Milne was to write between 1926 and 1928. However, in Christopher's 'nursery days' it was his Nanny, Olive Brockwell, the person employed to look after him, to whom he was most attached.

It was only after Nanny Brockwell left in 1929, when he was in his 9th year, said Christopher, that he and his father played games together. But paradoxically, it was during the time of Nanny Brockwell's incumbency that Milne wrote the four books featuring 'Christopher Robin' and 'Pooh', that would make him and his eponymously-named son famous throughout the world!

Christopher Robin Milne was born at 11 Mallord Street, Chelsea, London, on 21 August 1920. From the age of 6, Christopher attended Miss Walter's school in Tite Street, Chelsea, as did his childhood friend Anne Darlington.

'And we became countrymen', said Christopher:

'or, to be more accurate, half-countrymen. For we still spent most of our time in London, going down to Cotchford only at weekends and for the Easter and summer holidays. Up to then we had paid only occasional visits to the country. There had been visits to my mother's lovely family home of Brooklands on the Hamble [River, Hampshire], visits from which survive the memories of a rocking horse and -annually reawakened - the colour and scent of azaleas. There had been a holiday at Woolacombe [North Devon] where I had first encountered what I'm told I called "the huge water" and where - if anywhere - I had got "sand between the toes". There had been a famous holiday in Wales where the first poems of *When We Were Very Young* had been written. And finally, there had been visits to Decoy, a thatched cottage near Angmering in Sussex. At Decoy there was a lake. On the lake was a swan. And the swan's name was Pooh.'[1]

The name 'Pooh' was shortly to resonate all around the world, not as that of a swan, but of a bear! This was the result of Milne attaching the name 'Pooh', which was also the name of his son Christopher Robin's toy bear, to the name

'Winnie', hence, 'Winnie-the-Pooh'! As for 'Winnie', the origin of this name will be explained shortly.

In 1925, when Christopher was in his 5th year, his father had acquired Cotchford Farm near Hartfield in East Sussex:

'So there we were in 1925', said Christopher, at Cotchford Farm, 'with a cottage, a little bit of garden, a lot of jungle, two fields, a river and then all the green, hilly countryside beyond, meadows and woods, waiting to be explored; and Nanny and I set out at once to explore them, bringing back reports of our discoveries.'[2]

What of Nanny Brockwell? 'In the domestic hierarchy', said Christopher:

'nannies come somewhere in the middle. There were times when they would join the servants in the servants' quarters and times when they would join the gentry. But mostly their place was with their charge and that was in the nursery.' As regards their uniforms:

'There were black-and-white nannies, grey nannies, blue nannies and pink nannies. There were nannies with hats and nannies with veils. My nanny was grey, and she wore a veil when out in the street and a white cap and starched cuffs below when indoors.'

Referring to the Milnes' London home, said Christopher:

'We [i.e., he and Nanny Brockwell] lived together in a large nursery on the top floor. We lived there, played there, ate there - the food being brought up from the kitchen on a tray - and then at the end of the day we retired, each at our appointed time, to the night nursery next door.

So much were we together that Nanny became almost a part of me. Consequently, it was my occasional encounters with my parents that stand out as the events of the day.'

'Our first meeting would be after breakfast when I was allowed to visit the dining room. There was a large chest by the window and this was opened for me and I climbed inside while my father finished his marmalade and my mother ate her apple. Our next meeting was in the drawing-room after tea. In the drawing-room I could play on the sofa or on my father's armchair. One day, climbing about on the back of his chair, I fell off.'

'My final excursion was to the dining room in the evening. Here, on the floor under the table in the dark, I would play 'boofy games' with my mother, getting more and more excited until the arrival of Nanny would bring it all to an end and I would be swept upstairs to my bath.'[3]

Little did Christopher know that it was with the precise environment of Cotchford Farm in mind that his father would conjure up a parallel location for his most memorable creation, a bear named 'Pooh'!

'First we set off towards the river. We called it the river, though it was really only a stream, to distinguish it from the stream (at the bottom of the putting lawn) which was really only a long thin, almost stagnant pond.'[4]

'Posingford was a wood we often used to visit. It is about half a mile from end to end and runs uphill from the river at the bottom to the forest at the top. It is a gay and friendly wood, the sort of wood you could happily walk through at night, feeling yourself a skilful rather than a brave explorer: a wood of hazels and willows and sweet chestnuts with here and there an oak or a pine.'

'To the left of the path as it enters the wood is a lake. If you called our river a stream, then I suppose you would want to call this lake a bog.

But for me it was a lake. The path continues between lake and river until it is crossed by a larger track that has entered the wood over a bridge.

This bridge still stands and still looks much as it did when Shepard came there to draw it: it is Poohsticks Bridge.'[5]

This was a reference to the aforementioned illustrator E. H. Shepard, who was shortly to combine with Milne in the production of four of the most famous children's books ever published, books which many adults including the author of this narrative also thoroughly enjoyed. As for 'Poohsticks Bridge', this was soon to go down in the annals of English literature! The game of 'Poohsticks', 'which Pooh invented', was first mentioned in the story 'In which Pooh invents a New Game and Eeyore joins in' from *The House at Pooh Corner*, a Winnie-the-Pooh book by A. A. Milne. Each player drops a stick on one side of a bridge over a river or stream and the one whose stick first appears on the downstream is the winner.

'Some people are good with children, others are not', said Christopher. 'It is a gift. You either have it or you don't. My father didn't - not with children that is. Later on, it was different, very different. But I am thinking of nursery days. It was difficult for him, of course. For there was Nanny always in the way. Nanny who claimed so much of my affection. And on the rare occasions when Nanny was out of the room, there was my mother in her place. On Nanny's day off, there was Gertrude [the housemaid] looking after me. Where did he fit in? Nowhere special.' How sad this seems! But suddenly, a new character appeared on the scene. 'And now here was Soldier', said Christopher. 'Soldier' was a nickname for an acquaintance of Christopher's father.

'You could see how my eyes lit up at the very thought of Soldier, at the mere mention of his name. You could see (or you could be told) how he made me laugh, how I adored him. No, my father couldn't compete. Did this make him, I wonder, a little jealous, a little sad? Did he secretly envy those who had the gift? My poor father! All that was left to him were family visits to the London Zoo or family walks through the Sussex woods, and perhaps a few brief minutes of good-night story.'

Christopher's assertion, that his father was not good with children may have been true as a general rule, but by Christopher's own admission, his relationship with his father, once Nanny Brockwell was 'out of the way', was as close and loving as can possibly be imagined! Photographs taken at the time indicate that this was indeed the case. However, one day that loving relationship would sadly come to an end.

As for Christopher's 'nursery days', there is no doubt that Alan Milne would have loved to have played a greater role in the life of his infant son, which his self-confessed shyness evidently precluded him from doing.[6]

There were occasions, however, when the two did come together, and just how much Milne appreciated his son's company is revealed by this statement from Christopher:

'One of the first things a child discovers about a person is what he looks like - his face. My father's face was easiest in profile and that was how I used to draw it. He came up to the nursery and sat, smoking his pipe, at one end of the nursery table, while I sat at the other. He sat and smoked and thought. I sat and drew and occasionally rubbed out. We both sat in silence. This was something we did from time to time, something we could do together on our first shy meetings.'[7] The famous T. E. Lawrence (of Arabia) once remarked that if two people felt entirely comfortable in each other's presence, then there was no need for conversation.

On 15 January 1929, Christopher commenced at Gibbs School, an independent preparatory day school for boys near Sloane Square, London. 'I arrived at age eight-and-a-half', said Christopher, 'stayed for four terms, then went off to boarding school'.[8] In May 1930, Christopher started as a boarder at Boxgrove independent preparatory day school for boys near Guildford in Surrey. In 1933, when he was aged 13, he became a pupil at Stowe (public) School in Buckinghamshire.

Chapter 17

More About Christopher and His Father Alan

A measure of the lengths to which Alan Milne would go to make his son happy is indicated by Christopher, as follows:

'My nursery was in the front of the house facing the street. If I stood on the ottoman where I kept my toys, I could look through the bars of the window and see the whole length of Mallord Street below me.'[1]

'It was one of the most exciting moments in all our lives when the nursery door opened and a giant guardsman in full regalia with scarlet tunic and huge, furry busby strode into the room, marched up to the tiny boy and saluted.'

'The tiny boy was totally overcome; so much so that I cannot in the least recall what happened next. I imagine that I was allowed to hold his busby, even to try it on, to finger his buttons and epaulettes and all his accoutrements. Did I sit on his lap or ride on his back? Did he stay for tea? Did I cry when at last he said goodbye? But, of course, he would have promised to return; and he did - many, many times, though never again in scarlet. But he was always Soldier to me, indeed to us all.'

The 'guardsman' was, in fact, the actor and writer Louis Goodrich.

'He was, I believe, a casual acquaintance of my father's at the Garrick Club. One day, my father had been talking to him and had mentioned my current passion for the military, and Goodrich had said: "How would he like it if I dressed and came to see him?" And so, it was arranged. The day was set, the uniform hired, and thus began a long and close friendship between us.'

'Soldier', said Christopher:

'came to tea often - nursery tea, of course; for he came to see me, not my parents. He was such a very wonderful and exciting person that Anne was allowed to share him, and the four of us - Nanny, me, Soldier and Anne - had tea together.' This was a reference to Christopher's aforementioned friend Anne Darlington, who was 'eight months older than I was' and lived nearby.

The soldier guardsman would one day find an echo in Milne's poem 'Buckingham Palace', published in 1924 in the collection *When We Were Very Young*:

'They're changing guard at Buckingham Palace - Christopher Robin went down with Alice. Alice is marrying one of the guard. "A soldier's life is terrible hard",

Says Alice.'

'Alice', presumably, was Nanny Brockwell.

At Cotchford Farm, said Christopher:

'Putting, golf, cricket, catch, these were the things we did together - but not until Nanny had left us and I was at boarding school. Up to then, I was much like any other child in the country. I took my toys out and played with them in the grass. I played in the hay, I played in the mud, played in the water, played with friends, played with Nanny, played alone, climbed trees, picked primroses in the spring and nuts in the autumn, went exploring, rode a donkey.'[2]

Christopher described how, after the departure of Nanny Brockwell, he and Alan [A. A. Milne] would sit together on the sofa as his father showed him 'how one solved simultaneous equations'. Alan, it will be remembered, had graduated in mathematics from Cambridge University.

'So as we sat side by side, it was not of my future career that my father was thinking, but of the immediate present. For now, at long last, Nanny was out of the way. [As Christopher was due to go to boarding school, her services were presumably no longer required.] Now at last he and I could do things together. Here after ten years of waiting was his opportunity to share with me his boyhood enthusiasms, to relive his own boyhood through me, and in the process to find my love.'

'Would I stay with him a little longer to make up for those lost years? Till fourteen, perhaps, or sixteen? He was lucky. We were together until I was eighteen, very, very close. He knew he was lucky, that he had got perhaps more than he deserved, and he was very grateful. And once, a little shyly, he thanked me ….'

'Father and son. What sort of relationship is it?' asked Christopher:

'Does the father look down to the son, the son look up to the father? Or does the father get on to his hands and knees so that they are both on the same level? Sometimes the one, sometimes the other: but in our case neither would do. We had to be on the same level, but we both had to be standing, for my father couldn't bend, couldn't pretend to be what he wasn't. We would do algebra together, and Euclid, and look for birds' nests, and catch things in the stream, and play cricket in the meadow. We could putt on the lawn and throw tennis balls at each other. We could do those things as equals.'

'But what about those other moments, which adults pass in casual chit-chat, which husband and wife can so happily share in complete silence, content to be in each other's company? Meal times. Car journeys. After dinner in front of the fire.

Conversation with a small child is difficult. Perhaps, instead, one might learn the Morse code. My father had learnt it during the war when he was battalion signals officer. So now he taught me and with hand squeezes we were able to pass messages to each other as Burnside [presumably the chauffeur] drove us down to Cotchford.'

'Then at lunch time mightn't I feel a bit left out if he and my mother discussed dull, grown-up things?[3] So, "How about a game?" he would say, and we would play clumps, or go through the alphabet to see how many flowers we could name beginning with each letter in turn.'

In the game of 'clumps', one person or team thinks of a word or thing and the other asks them questions to discover what it is.

In respect of his future, said Christopher: 'My father never wanted me to be a writer. An artist, perhaps. An architect, perhaps. But not a writer. This great talent was all his own and not to be shared. Anyway, a ten-year-old schoolboy doesn't need to be thinking about his career just yet. Other things come first. Cricket, for instance.'

'Cricket, like football, is a game you can either play or (equally happily) watch. My father did both. He did most of his watching at the Oval, and as soon as I was old enough, I accompanied him. I was about ten or eleven, and, if I remember, Woolley was batting at the time.'[4] The Oval, a cricket ground in Kennington, Lambeth, south London, had been the home ground of Surrey County Cricket Club since it opened in 1845. Frank E. Woolley, was a batsman for Kent County Cricket Club and England.

'We lived in Chelsea and so should by rights have backed Middlesex, but my father's allegiance as a Londoner was always to Surrey. When we bought Cotchford he transferred most of it to Sussex; and I was for Sussex, too, wholeheartedly.'[5]

Christopher described how his shyness, together with the 'jamming' of his words when he spoke (presumably a stutter) made him avoid entering shops. Many fathers would have become impatient with this, but not so Milne.

'What does a parent do in such circumstances? Does he (for example) say "If you want it, you must go and buy it yourself"? Or does he say "All right, let's go and buy it together"? Rightly or wrongly, it was the latter that my father did, and I blessed him for it and loved him all the more'.[6]

When Nanny Brockwell left, Christopher said: 'I was still as shy as ever; worse, if anything. I still needed someone to cling to.' This was even though he was now 9 years old:

'So I clung to my father. For nearly ten years I had clung to Nanny. For nearly ten more years I was to cling to him, adoring him as I had adored Nanny, so that he too became almost a part of me, at first, no doubt, to his delight, later perhaps to his anxiety.'[7]

'So there I was, very close indeed to my father, adoring him, admiring him, accepting his ideas, yet at the same time immensely sensitive, easily wounded, quick to take offence. An accidental word of reproof or criticism from him and tears would stream from my eyes and a barrier of silence would descend between us keeping us apart for days. So he had to be careful what he said.'[8] Over-sensitivity was indeed one of Christopher's weaknesses, as will be seen.

Christopher described how his father Alan relived his own childhood vicariously through his son:

'My father, who had derived such happiness from his childhood, found in me the companion with whom he could return there. When I was three, he was three. When I was six, he was six. We grew up side by side, and as we grew so the books were written.' And when Christopher was nine and Nanny left:

'We could now do real things together: reality could in part replace the dream. For the next nine years we continued to grow up alongside each other. I was not aware of this, of course. I just saw him as my father. But he, I now suspect, saw me as a sort of twin brother, perhaps a sort of reincarnation of Ken.'[9]

This was a reference to Milne's older brother Kenneth ('Ken'), who had died of tuberculosis, age 19, on 21 May 1929, and Milne had revealed his deep love for his late brother by dedicating his autobiography *It's Too Late Now* to him:

1880 – 1929 TO THE MEMORY OF KENNETH JOHN MILNE WHO BORE THE WORST OF ME AND MADE THE BEST OF ME

'I - as I have already mentioned - needed him', Christopher continued. 'He no less but for a different reason needed me. He needed me to escape from being fifty.'[10]

'In front of the house a lawn sloped down to a ditch. It was virtually the only lawn that Cotchford possessed when we first arrived, and at once my father claimed it as his own private preserve and laid it out for clock golf. And as a clock golf course it always remained, the only bit of the garden where my father reigned supreme. The ditch that bounded its lower edge was widened and turned into a moat, known as "the stream".'

'The putting lawn remained unchanged over the years, and round and round it my father went, round and round and round. If I was at home, I joined him. "Just time for a quick record [i.e., beating the record for the lowest score!] before lunch?" We played together, not against each other: more friendly that way.'

'If I wasn't there, he played alone; and if he did a particularly good round, he would proudly tell me.' This happy state of affairs continued even when Christopher went away to boarding school:

My father 'would tell me in his weekly letter. He didn't tell my mother: she wouldn't have been specially interested, wouldn't even have known what "two under twos" meant. She never played.

She hated all games.'[11]

Christopher described how his parents complemented one another:

'So while my mother dug, my father putted. Does this sound like ant and grasshopper? In a way it was. But you can look at it another way. To each his trade. My father was a writer: this was his work. All he wanted from my mother was her encouragement and praise. My mother was a gardener, and praise and encouragement was all she wished for in return. No need also for a hand with the manuring: we had a full-time professional for that.'[12]

Another source of delight, said Christopher, was the stream:

'We plunged nets and golf clubs into it, and piles of weed with their attendant black mud were landed on the bank. We stooped to peer closely.

And gradually the various inhabitants would work their way up to the surface, flip-flapping if they were fish, wriggling if they were newts, crawling if they were dragonfly larvae.'[13]

'Once we had moved down to Cotchford, though we would listen to the Test Match on the wireless - my father in the garden suddenly remembering, looking at his watch, giving a shout, galloping indoors, me following, enthusiastic, but with my enthusiasm never quite matching his - and though we would excitedly follow the fortunes of Sussex in the papers, we would never watch another first-class match. Why was this? Partly, I think, it was because he didn't want to have more than his fair share of me. If I was with him, then I was not with my mother. I played golf with him in the morning, I putted with him, played catch with him, and then in the evening we bowled at each other in the meadow. This was already almost more than his ration; and so, much as he might have liked to take me up to London to watch Surrey playing Sussex, it would have been wrong to do so.'[14] Here, Christopher is alluding to his father Alan's unselfishness.

As a former member of J. M. Barrie's Allahakbarries cricket team, it is not surprising that Milne introduced the game to his young son.

'Cricket could be played in the meadow and catch with a tennis ball up against the wall. So my father was determined that, however much I enjoyed just being in the country, playing happily by myself, doing nothing happily by myself, however cat-like I was, I was jolly well going to spend some of my time enjoying dog games with him.'[15]

'Cotchford was built on a hillside and so almost everything was on a slope. But there was one level bit, a grass path that, starting off between two giant yews, ran through what we called the orchard. Five feet wide, twenty yards long, and absolutely straight, it would serve admirably.'

It was in Nanny Brockwell's time, said Christopher, 'that I first took up my stance, while my father bowled at me with a tennis ball and Nanny stood at deep cover point to retrieve anything that went down the hill towards the dovecot.'[16]

'On summer evenings I changed into my white flannels (my first long trousers), put on pads and gloves, collected bat and ball, and off we went together. I batted, he bowled. And sometimes an off drive, slightly lofted to clear the thick grass, would almost reach the river; but more often a sweep to leg, flying over the net, would land in the swamp by the willows. "Oh, well hit! Quick!" and we would rush to the spot and tramp up and down among the rushes, while horseflies hovered overhead.'

'Cricket was for summer evenings, and afterwards there was a tray with a jug of lemonade waiting in the dining-room. But catch with a tennis ball, like putting, was for the odd five minutes while waiting for Pat [the cook] to ring the bell for lunch.'[17]

In his book *The Enchanted Places*, Christopher made several statements in respect of his father, that do not seem to quite tally with the close and loving relationship between the two of them that he himself described. In *The Enchanted Places*, Christopher stated as follows:

'People sometimes say to me today: "How lucky you were to have had such a wonderful father!" imagining that because he wrote about me with such affection and understanding, he must have played with me with equal affection and understanding. Can this really be so totally untrue? Isn't this most surprising? No, it is not really surprising, not when you understand.'
'There are two sorts of writer. There is the writer who is basically a reporter and there is the creative writer. The one draws on his experiences, the other on his dreams. My father was a creative writer and so it was precisely because he was not able to play with his small son that his longings sought and found satisfaction in another direction. He wrote about him instead.'[18]

Here, Christopher is apparently contradicting himself because he had already explained that the reason his father had not played with him was because of the presence of Nanny Brockwell, and not because he was a creative writer. In other words, Christopher was in denial about the true extent of his father's great and enduring love for him.

However, once Nanny had departed the scene, Alan Milne did play with his son and not only that, he revelled in the boy's company, to an extent that most children would have envied!

Above: Roger Gilbert Lancelyn Green, circa 1987. (Photo by kind permission of Scirard Lancelyn Green)

Right: J. M. Barrie, 1892. (National Media Museum)

Sir Arthur Conan Doyle, 27 January 1913. (George Grantham Bain Collection, The Library of Congress)

Members of the Allahakbarries XI and E. V. Lucas's XI, Downe House, July 1913: Back row, l to r: George Llewelyn Davies, Thomas L. Gilmour, Will Meredith, George Meredith junior, Denis Mackail, Harry Graham, Dr Ernest Goffe. Centre row, l to r, A. A. Milne, Maurice Hewlett, J. M. Barrie, George Morrow, E. V. Lucas, Walter Frith. Front row, l to r: Percy Lucas, Audrey Lucas, T. Wrigley, Charles Tennyson, Willie Winter. This was the final game played by the Allahakbarries.

'At 13:30 hrs on 3 October 1917, during the Battle of Passchendaele, 'Pigeon 2709' [of the British Army] was despatched to take a signal to brigade HQ. The flight should have only taken 20 minutes, but soon after setting off '2709' was hit by enemy fire. The bullet broke a leg and passed out of his body, leaving the small metal message cylinder embedded in his side. Although it took him a further 21 agonising hours, '2709' completed his mission. The message was delivered at 10:30 hrs the next morning, but Pigeon 2709 died shortly afterwards.' Kendall-Carpenter, Nick, *Roger So Far: The First 100 years of the Royal Corps of Signals*, p.24.

Above: A. A. Milne (front row, 4th from right) with other Signals Instructors at Portsmouth Garrison Signalling School, 1917. (Royal Signals Museum, Blandford Camp, Blandford Forum, Dorset, UK)

Left: Signals Officer A. A. Milne, 1917. (Royal Signals Museum, Blandford Camp, Blandford Forum, Dorset, UK)

War Office,
Whitehall,
S.W.

PRIVATE & CONFIDENTIAL.

Dear Sir,

I beg to thank you for your letter, giving information about yourself with reference to literary and journalistic work. This information will be filed for reference by M.I.7b.

You are no doubt aware that our enemies have a very extensive propaganda organization, of which they have made effective use in most parts of the world during the whole period of the present war.

Among the officers now serving with His Majesty's Forces there are some who are qualified to give valuable assistance in the work of counteracting propaganda emanating from enemy sources, which is calculated to injure the causes and interests of the Allies. It is believed that many such officers now serving in Home Commands would be very glad to assist in this work, if they found they were able to do so without interference with their present duties. The practicability of this can only be tested by actual trial.

To that end, I am permitted to suggest to you that you might send me an article, preferably one of about 1,000, or 1,200 words, and certainly not exceeding 2,000 words, dealing in a popular way, and descriptively rather than opinionatively, with any aspect of the war which appeals to you personally, in a manner which you consider would be helpful to the Allied cause. Such an article should be suitable for publication in the Press. For purposes of propaganda, and the information of our own public and the peoples of other countries, regarding the Allies' part in the war, what may be called the human interest is the most important; descriptive work is always valuable; strategy and tactics are out of place.

The field is a wide one, and in suggesting your contribution of a specimen article, your freedom in the matter of choice of subject is in no way restricted; it being obvious that your writing is likely to be more effective if its subject is an aspect of war interests which appeals especially to yourself, than if any particular line were indicated to you.

Yours faithfully,

G Dawson

Captain, M.I.7b.

Letter from the War Office inviting literati such as A. A. Milne to join British Military Intelligence Department MI7B.

The King's Breakfast, 1928 Edition.

A. A. Milne and Christopher Robin Milne. (*Illustrated London News Ltd*/Mary Evans. Was there ever a more loving photograph of father and his son?)

Above left: Dorothy ('Daphne') Milne. (Mary Evans Picture Library)

Above right: Christopher Robin Milne and Winnie-the-Pooh. (Everett Collection/ Mary Evans. The sheer size of Christopher's toy bear may come as a surprise!)

Right: A. A. Milne, September 1922, by Emile Otto Hoppe. (*Wikimedia Commons*)

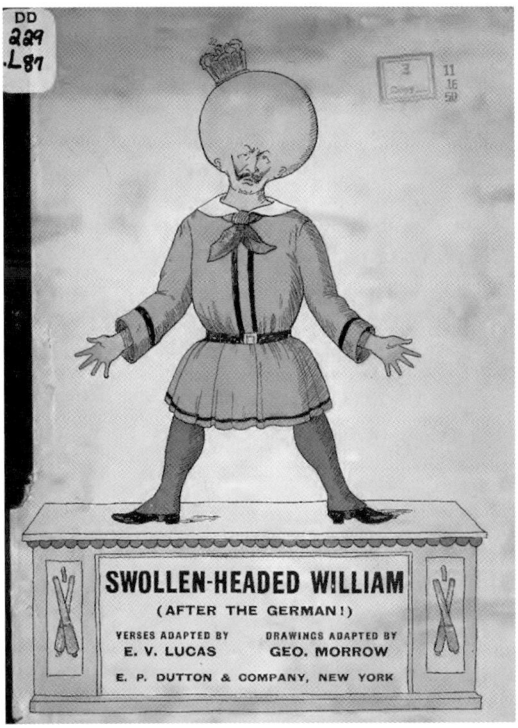

Above left: Edward Verrall Lucas, circa 1905. (*Wikimedia Commons*)

Above right: Ernest Howard Shepard by Gwen Morgan, rights owner unknown. (National Portrait Gallery)

Left: *Swollen-Headed William; Painful Stories and Funny Pictures after the German* by E. V. Lucas. (*Wikimedia Commons*)

Christopher Robin Milne and six year old Jeannie Cutting. (Keystone Pictures USA/ ZUMAPRESS.com/Mary Evans)

Left: Harry Colebourn and 'Winnie', 1914, Manitoba Provincial Archives. (*Wikimedia Commons*)

Below: Officers and men of the 2nd Canadian Infantry Brigade with Harry Colebourn (2nd row, 2nd from left) and 'Winnie' in front row. (Lindsay Mattick via AP/ Canadian Press)

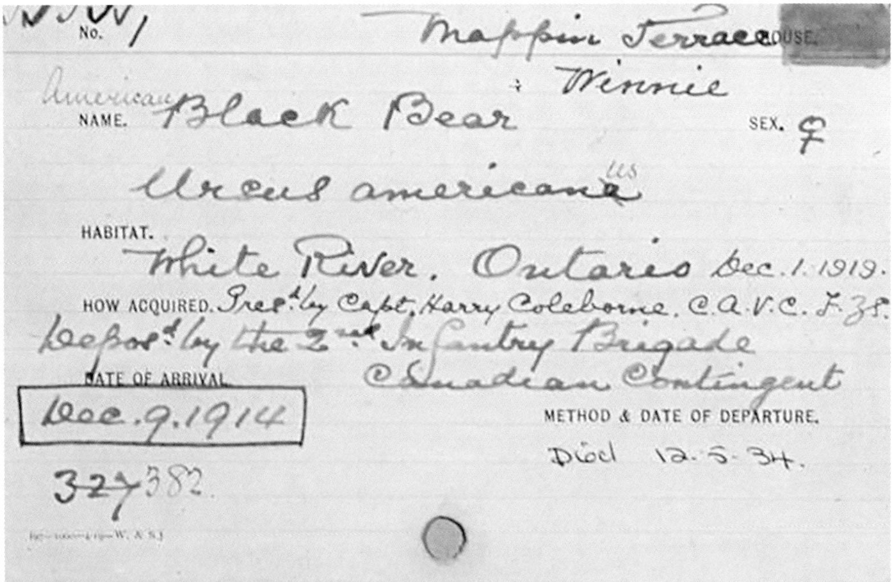
No. 1 Mappin Terrace HOUSE.
Winnie
NAME. American Black Bear SEX. ♀
Ursus americanus
HABITAT. White River, Ontario
HOW ACQUIRED. Presd by Capt. Harry Colebourne. C.A.V.C.
Depos'd by the 2nd Infantry Brigade Canadian Contingent
DATE OF ARRIVAL Dec. 9. 1914
METHOD & DATE OF DEPARTURE. Died 12. 5. 34.
382

Record Card for 'Winnie'. (London Zoo)

Original Winnie-the-Pooh stuffed toys. Clockwise from bottom left: Tigger, Kanga, Edward Bear (a.k.a Winnie-the-Pooh), Eeyore, and Piglet. Roo was also one of the original toys, but he was lost during the 1930s in an apple orchard somewhere in Sussex. Owl and Rabbit were not based on toys. Gopher was made up for the Disney version. New York Public Library. (*Wikimedia Commons*)

Winnie-the-Pooh and friends, watercolour painting by E. H. Shepard. (Art Collection, Harry Ransom Center, The University of Texas at Austen, USA)

Statue of Harry Colebourn and 'Winnie' by Bill Epp, presented to London Zoo by the people of Manitoba through their Government on 19th July 1995.

Left: Christopher Robin Milne and his fiancée Lesley de Sélincourt, 21 April 1948. (Keystone Pictures USA/ZUMAPRESS.com/Mary Evans)

Below: Postage stamp based on animated film 'Winnie-the-Pooh', derived from the children's book by Alan Milne, translated by Boris Zakhoder, 18 February 1988. USSR post. (*Wikimedia Commons*)

A group of poets: Standing, left to right: Mark Gertler, Hewy Levy, Walter J. Turner, Alan Alexander Milne. Seated, left to right: Ralph Hodgson, J. W. N. Sullivan and S. S. Koteliansky, 1928. (*Wikimedia Commons*)

A. A. Milne & E. H. Shephard memorial plaque. 'And by and by they came to an enchanted place on the very top of the Forest called Galleons Lap.' (Nigel Freeman)

Nancy and Jack Norman, grandchildren of the author, in Selfridges Department Store, London, with 'Pooh' toys! (Thomas Norman)

Chapter 18

Christopher and His Mother Dorothy ('Daphne')

'Provided Nanny was at hand in case of difficulty', said Christopher, Daphne (his mother) 'was very happy to spend an occasional half hour with me, playing on the floor, sitting me on her lap to show me how the gentleman rides, reciting (for the hundredth time) [poet] Edward Lear's "Calico Pie".'

'I enjoyed playing with my mother. This was something she was good at. There were plenty of things she couldn't do, had never been taught to do, didn't need to do because there was someone to do them for her and she certainly couldn't have coped alone.'[1]

'My mother had been brought up partly in London, partly in the country. She knew what it was to live in a large country house and sit on lawns and wander past flower beds. London, no doubt, attracted her, especially as she grew older, with its gay parties and its pretty clothes, with its opportunity to escape from her wretched brothers [Aubrey, Geoffrey, and Guy] and their muddy knees and everlasting sailing-talk. But at Brooklands [Daphne's family's country home in Hampshire] her deep and abiding love of gardens was born and with it her love of the peace and the solitude that you can find only in the country.'[2]

Christopher recalled his mother:

'in her garden, trowel in hand planting Darwin tulips [named after biologist Charles Darwin] by the hundred. Secateurs in hand snipping at roses. Crouched down, weeding, weeding, weeding. Pouring jugs of hot water over the ants. Exhorting Tasker [the gardener] to ever greater efforts. Teaching me the names of the flowers - lovely names like *salpiglossis* and *spiraea Anthony Waterer*, difficult names like *eschscholtzia* which were fun to spell. But mostly I remember her just quietly, happily, brooding over it all, alone in the half dark.'

'You can love the country in two quite different ways, as a cat loves it and as a dog loves it. My mother was like a cat. She responded to the beauty, the peace and the solitude that it offered. She found this in her garden and she found it too in the countryside beyond. Solitude. She was happiest alone. Once, when she was going for a walk, I asked if I could come with her. "No", she said, "but come and meet me on my way back. I like best being met".'[3]

'At night, before going to bed, she would walk up to the forest, two miles along the road, until she was level with Gill's Lap [a viewpoint in Ashdown Forest]. On these occasions I sometimes accompanied her. It was different in the dark.

You could be with someone and they would be there if you felt you wanted them, and if you didn't you could forget them.'[4]

From the above account, it is clear that Christopher was as devoted to his mother as he was to his father.

'We both loved the country at night, the black shapes of the trees, the tiny spots of light from wayside cottages, the sound of the wind bustling about its invisible business. We scarcely talked, absorbed in our private thoughts.'

'If my mother was a cat, my father was surely a dog. He was a Londoner, a real Londoner with a deep love of London in his bones. For him the country had always been, not where you lived but where you went. Where you went on holiday. Where you went to do something - to ride a bicycle, to climb a hill, to look for birds' nests, to play golf. Like a dog, he couldn't just be in the country, sitting or strolling aimlessly. It had to be a proper walk, a walk with a purpose, planned beforehand, worked out on the map even. And you couldn't go alone; you had to be with somebody, with me perhaps, or with the whole family, Nanny included. Like a dog, too, he was happiest of all when chasing a ball.'[5]

Here, Christopher highlighted the fact that, whereas his mother Daphne was of a solitary nature, his father Alan needed company.

Chapter 19

What Motivated Milne to Write?

In his book *The Enchanted Places*, Christopher described the outcome of an interview which took place when a journalist called 'Miss Brown' [not her real name] came to visit his father in the summer of 1932. 'The main point' which Miss Brown established, said Christopher, 'was that Mr Milne took his writing very seriously, even though he "was taking it into [i.e., writing about] the nursery" as he put it.' But what were Milne's priorities when he wrote?

'There was no question of tossing off something that was good enough for the kiddies. He was writing first to please and satisfy himself.

After that he wanted to please his wife. He depended utterly upon doing this. Without her encouragement, her delight and her laughter he couldn't have gone on. With it who cared what the critics wrote or how few copies Methuen sold?

Then he hoped to please his boy. This came third, not first, as so many people supposed.'[1]

'Did Christopher Robin or Mrs Milne help him with ideas?', Miss Brown enquired of Milne. 'Yes and no, it seemed', Christopher continued:

'There was the Forest and the Five Hundred Acre Wood. These were real. Then there were the animals. They were real, too (except for Owl and Rabbit that he had invented). His wife and his boy (always his boy, never Christopher. Odd!) had, as it were, breathed life into them, given them their characters. What he had done was to write stories round them. The stories were entirely his own invention.'

'Miss Brown' remarked that Milne's books 'seemed to show a great understanding and love of children. Was he very fond of children?' To this, Milne responded first with silence. Then he said:

'I am not inordinately fond of them, if that is what you mean, and I have certainly never felt in the least sentimental about them or no more sentimental than one becomes for a moment over a puppy or a kitten. In as far as I understand them, this understanding is based on observation, on imagination and on memories of my own childhood.'[2]

Sentimental is defined as 'of or prompted by feelings of tenderness, sadness, or nostalgia'.[3] Yes, granted, Milne may have felt unsentimental about other people's children, but in respect of his son Christopher, he felt the utmost love and tenderness. So much is evident from Christopher's own account. As for Milne, it was surely with his son in mind that he wrote his poem '*Vespers*':

'Little Boy kneels at the foot of the bed,
Droops on the little hands little gold head.
Hush! Hush! Whisper who dares!
Christopher Robin is saying his prayers.

God bless Mummy. I know that's right.
Wasn't it fun in the bath tonight?
The cold's so cold, and hot's so hot.
Oh! God bless Daddy – I quite forgot.

There is another reason why Milne may have derived satisfaction from writing his

'Winnie-the-Pooh' books. As already mentioned, he had served in the First World War and his subsequent nervous behaviour strongly suggests that he was suffering from post-traumatic stress disorder, in which he would have experienced 'flashbacks' – disturbing, sudden, vivid memories of what he had witnessed on the battlefield. In creating the relatively safe world of Pooh, this may have been a therapy for him, and it also may have been a therapy for Shepard, who also served in that terrible war.

Miss Brown asked another question of Milne: 'What does your son think about it all now? How has it affected him, being, you might almost say, a household name?' Said Christopher, 'Mr Milne had answered this question rather more slowly, rather more thoughtfully, perhaps rather less confidently. He hoped it had done him no harm, might even have done some good, His boy seemed perfectly happy and was certainly doing very well at school and enjoying it all. He didn't think he would ever grow up to wish his name was Charles Robert.'[4] In other words, for Christopher to wish that he was somebody else.

Alas, Christopher Robin Milne must have wished on innumerable occasions that his father had not chosen to call the fictional owner of

'Winnie-the-Pooh' 'Christopher Robin', especially when, the year after 'Miss Brown' had interviewed his father, Christopher was sent to Stowe School where he endured severe bullying on this account, as will shortly be seen!

Chapter 20

Milne and Shepard Meet (Autumn 1923): E. V. Lucas - The Catalyst

In handwritten notes made in 1956, the illustrator E. H. Shepard stated as follows:

'One Wednesday evening late in the autumn of 1923 I was sitting next to E. V. Lucas at our weekly *Punch* dinner. Besides being an author, Lucas was also chairman of Methuen the publishers. He turned to me and said, quite casually, "Ernest, we have some charming poems for children sent to us by A. A. Milne and we want to publish them.

Would you like to illustrate them?" I said "Yes" without a moment's hesitation for though I did not know Milne (he had given up coming to the *Punch* table by that time) of course I was familiar with his writing. That was my introduction to *When We Were Very Young*. I did not have to wait long before the first poems reached me, among them "*Teddy Bear*" and "*The King's Breakfast*" and I realised what a grand time was ahead of me.'

Furthermore, Milne told Shepard that when his next book was published, "I should like you to illustrate it".[1] However, Milne admitted that initially, he had failed to recognise E. H. Shepard's qualities and potential as an illustrator. He said:

'In those early days before the war, when he [Shepard] was making his first tentative pictures for *Punch*, I used to say to F. H. [Frederick Henry] Townsend, the Art Editor, on the occasion of each new Shepard drawing, "What on earth do you see in this man? He's perfectly hopeless", and Townsend would say complacently, "You wait." So I waited.'

Milne asked himself, was 'Townsend 'a man of remarkable insight' or was he himself 'just an ordinary fool'? And Milne concluded that Townsend 'was something of' the former, and he 'more than a little' of the latter.[2]

Lucas described Shepard, who was subsequently to become 'Milne's collaborator with the pencil', as being 'notable for the charm of his fantasies'.[3] As for Lucas, in his autobiography *Reading, Writing and Remembering* (published in 1932) he praised Milne to the skies:

'Not since its foundation in 1841 has *Punch*, in my opinion, printed articles of such unwavering high spirits, fun and felicity of phrase as those signed "A. A. M." A new kind of nonsense was his, based upon and blended with the facts of life, never permitting an intruding qualm, and all carried out with apparently effortless ease and the utmost gaiety.'

'The art that conceals art. Anyone sitting down to the portmanteau volume *Those Were The Days*, in which his weekly articles are collected, must agree with me. Portions of *When We Were Very Young* appeared in *Punch* too, but long after his retirement.'[4]

Chapter 21

More About E. H. Shepard

Brilliant as Milne's poems and stories are, including those featuring 'Pooh', they were raised to a sublimer level by the illustrations created by E. H. Shepard. What, apart from a creative instinct, did Shepard and Milne have in common? This will become evident from the following narrative.

Just as Milne had struggled to become an established writer, so Shepard had struggled to become an established illustrator. So much is evident from his autobiography *Drawn From Life* (published in 1961). And yet, judging by the awards that he won, Shepard was a star pupil!

Ernest Howard Shepard was born at number 55, Springfield Road, St John's Wood, London, on 10 December 1879. He was therefore three years older than A. A. Milne. Shepard's father Henry Dunkin Shepard was an architect, married to (Harriet) Jessie (née Lee). He had two older siblings, sister Ethel Shepard (born 1877) and brother Cyril Harry Shepard (born 1878). Shortly after his birth, the family relocated to 10 Kent Terrace near Regent's Park.[1]

'Mother always encouraged my drawing', said Shepard:

'and, though she had little talent herself, would show me how to use my paints. We made plans together for when I grew up and became an artist myself. She, almost more than Father, inspired me to persevere.'[2]

In 1890, when Shepard was only ten, his mother Jessie died, whereupon he and his siblings were sent to live with their five maiden aunts in London's Gordon Square, Bloomsbury, where they remained for almost a year.[3]

Shepard and his brother Cyril now attended an elementary school in Baker Street where, he declared, he spent 'four happy years'.[4] The brothers subsequently became day pupils at St John's Wood Preparatory School (nicknamed 'Olivers') in Acacia Road.[5] Here, he said, 'I do not remember learning anything at all beyond an apprenticeship in self-preservation'.[6]

The family subsequently relocated to Theresa Terrace, Hammersmith.[7] The brothers were now to spend several terms at St Paul's Preparatory School, Colet Court (nicknamed 'Bewsher's') at Barnes, prior to entering St Paul's senior school.[8]

After his mother's death, Shepard said:

'I missed her companionship terribly and determined to justify her faith in my talent. So, I was particularly glad when Father told me he had taken a studio and that I should be able to practice in it.'

Henry Shepard was an architectural adviser to University College Hospital, 'and for convenience he rented the studio in Gower Street'. Henry was also an amateur watercolourist. 'It was on the first floor, over an artists' colourman [person who deals in artists' paints]'s shop, where the students from the Slade School [of Fine Art, Gower Street, London] came to buy their paints. I made a habit of going there to do my lessons. Carrying my drawing-book, I would spend hours at work there.'[9]

Furthermore, Royal Academician Frank Dicksee, who was a friend of his father, invited Shepard to his studio in Peel Street and encouraged him to try his hand at painting in oils.[10]

All work and no play makes Jack a dull boy, so the saying goes, and Shepard described how his father took him and his brother Cyril to see his first cricket match, where the 'redoubtable Dr W. G.' was in action![11] This was William Gilbert Grace, medical practitioner and former captain of England whose cricket career spanned over fifty years! Also, Shepard recalled how during one Christmas holiday, he and his siblings were taken by their father to a Christmas pantomime at the Crystal Palace.[12]

'In due course the Shepard family moved to Ravenscourt Park in West London, partly to be closer to St Paul's School, where the two boys could be day pupils. Shepard began his formal education at Colet Court, the preparatory school for St Paul's, before moving up to the main school.[13]

In 1892, at the age of 12, Shepard became a pupil at St Paul's School, his older brother Cyril having commenced there a year earlier. At the school, where Shepard's paternal uncle William ('Willie') was a master, Shepard was 'put into the special drawing class', of which he was the only member![14] In 1895, during his final year at St Paul's, he said, he 'had quite definitely settled' that he 'would be an artist. This pleased Father and he gave me every encouragement.' As for Shepard's siblings, Ethel became a church of England missionary and Cyril became a solicitor.[15]

In 1896, Shepard enrolled for Saturday study at the Heatherley School of Fine Art, Chelsea. This 'was chosen from among the many arts schools because Father had once attended evening classes there'.[16]

In 1897, having been awarded a scholarship, Shepard 'was accepted at the Royal Academy Schools with three years free tuition.[17] Every half-year there was a scholarship examination at the schools and a fresh influx of students'.[18]

The Royal Academy of Arts, Burlington House, Piccadilly, London, is 'an independent, privately funded institution led by eminent artists and architects. Its purpose is to promote the creation, enjoyment and appreciation of the visual arts through exhibitions, education and debate'[19] The Royal Academy of Arts includes the Royal Academy Schools, which were created to provide professional training for artists in the UK.

It was while he was a student there, said Shepard, that he first set eyes on Florence Eleanor Chaplin:

'I was copying the [painting of] Philip of Spain by Velázquez when she came in with another girl and stood watching me at work. I had heard her spoken of as being one of the cleverest students, a distinction she shared with Flora Lion.' Flora became a distinguished portrait painter. 'Florence Chaplin's talent was inherited from her grandfather, Ebenezer Landells, the artist and engraver and one of the founders of *Punch*.'[20] So here we have yet another connection with *Punch* magazine! Shepard continued:

'Second-year students who had passed into the Upper [Royal Academy] School and could show a record of regular attendance and good behaviour were given certain privileges. Amongst these was the chance to compete for a scholarship called

"The Landseer" which was worth £40 a year for two years.'

Painter and former Keeper at the Royal Academy Charles Landseer, who died in 1879, had bequeathed the sum of £10,000 to fund scholarships for painting and sculpture.

'Without telling Father I entered three works - a study of a head, a painting of a nude, and a drawing. It was a pleasant surprise for him, as for me, when I won the scholarship.'[21]

Shepard said: 'In the early part of the summer I devoted some weeks to working for a British Institution prize.' The British Institution was founded in 1805 in order to promote the Fine Arts in the UK.

'This was a cash prize of £60 a year for two years and was open to students all over the kingdom. When the results were declared in July, I was one of the lucky ones. This, added to my £40 from the Landseer Scholarship, would give me £100 for the next year, and I began to consider the possibility of taking a studio in town, perhaps sharing it with another student.'

Shepard, together with fellow student George Swaish, a future portrait and figure painter, subsequently rented number 52, Glebe Place, in Chelsea:

'It was large with enough space for two to work. It had a tiny bedroom, big enough for two truckle beds, an adequate lavatory, a larder, and a coalhole. The rent was £50 per annum.'[22]

'The prize distribution at the Academy Schools that winter was a really happy event for me. I had won a medal for a painted figure and ten pounds for a set of life drawings. But what pleased me even more was that Florence Chaplin had won the £40 prize for a mural.'[23] The mural was entitled 'The Procession of the Hours'.

Clearly, Shepard was quite taken with Florence!

In 1901, Shepard's Landseer Scholarship expired, whereupon he said:

I 'was no longer compelled to work every day at the Schools. I spent more time at Glebe Place making black-and-white drawings. Then I received a commission to illustrate *Tom Brown's Schooldays* [a novel by Thomas Hughes, set in the 1830s in Rugby School]. I had a copy of the original edition (my prize won at "Bewsher's") with the fine illustrations by [painters and illustrators] Arthur Hughes and Sydney P. Hall, and I found it difficult to avoid being unduly influenced by them.'[24]

In that year of 1901, Shepard 'had two pictures accepted for the Royal Academy Summer Exhibition and one, a portrait of his sister Ethel, was hung on the line – a phrase still used at the Royal Academy to mark the prestigious positioning of a work at eye level'.[25]

In 1902, Shepard's father Henry died at the age of 56, whereupon the family home was sold and Shepard and his siblings 'moved into rooms in Hyde Vale close to the Heath'.[26] This was Blackheath, in Kent.

'Part of my time at Blackheath was spent in looking for subjects to paint and I found some in Morden College.' This was a charitable institution, founded in 1695 by merchant and philanthropist Sir John Morden, which was dedicated to the care of the elderly. 'The little chapel appealed to me particularly and I promised myself I would paint it when circumstances permitted.'

In the spring of 1902, said Shepard, Florence Chaplin (who he nicknamed 'Pie'), 'was commissioned to carry out her prize mural design in the nurses' dining room at Guy's Hospital'.[27] Referring to Florence, to whom he was now engaged, Shepard described:

'the courage of a girl who was prepared to share the life of a penniless artist. I was earning something with my black-and-white drawings, though my efforts to get a drawing accepted by *Punch* were fruitless: it was two years before I achieved that.'

Meanwhile, he said, 'I spent part of every day working on my picture in the chapel at Morden College'.[28]

Having heard that the Academy had accepted his picture, said Shepard:

'a varnishing ticket followed. Varnishing day was a great occasion, when artists were able to see their accepted pictures in the galleries - the lucky ones hung on the line.'

'I met several friends and one of them told me that Edwin Abbey was in one of the galleries.' This was Edwin Austin Abbey, an American muralist, illustrator, and painter. 'I promptly went in search of him and found him deep in conversation with a fellow Royal Academician. I waited till presently he saw me and greeted me with: "Hallo, Shepard, what are you doing here?" I told him and he went on: "You should go on with your black and white, you know. Have you tried *Punch*?" I told him of my unsuccessful efforts. "You must meet [Edward] Linley Sambourne [cartoonist and illustrator], he said. "He's somewhere about.

Come along and I'll introduce you." He took my arm and we charged from room to room.'

'Sambourne was talking to a friend. He was the senior cartoonist for *Punch*, having taken John Tenniel's place three years earlier.' Illustrator, graphic humourist and political cartoonist for *Punch*, Sir John Tenniel was famous for illustrating Lewis Carroll's 'Alice' books. 'He turned towards us while Abbey, holding my arm, said: "Here, Sambourne, do you know Shepard? A promising young artist who wants to get into *Punch*". Then he gave me a dig as though to say, "Now get on with it", and left us.'

Thereafter Frank Dicksee informed Shepard that he and sculptor Sir William Hamo Thornycroft had:

'"been deputed to buy a picture for a colonial art gallery and we both would like to buy yours. We can only spend £100 - can you sell it for that?" My voice, I fear, was hardly audible. "Yes", I said, "I shall be very glad to. Thank you so much". Frank then said: "I expect you'll find the money useful when you get married". I was able to answer heartily, "Indeed we shall!" A hundred pounds was more than I should have dared to ask.'[29]

Now, Shepard could go ahead and rent a cottage for himself and Florence at Shamley Green near Guildford in Surrey. On 28 September 1904, the pair were married. In 1907 she bore him a son, Graham, and in 1909 a daughter, Mary.

'Shepard regularly sent cartoons, drawings, and illustrations speculatively to a variety of publications, including *Punch* magazine, and received frequent rejections. But gradually he built up a practice from a portfolio of publishers, principally for periodicals but also for book illustrations. He worked at home in a small studio in the garden at Shamley Green and would use a Triumph motorbike to get to Guildford station and commute into London whenever necessary.'[30]

By 1906, Shepard had become a successful illustrator, having produced work for illustrated editions of *Aesop's Fables*, *David Copperfield*, and *Tom Brown's Schooldays*, while at the same time working as an illustrator on the staff of *Punch* (from 1921).[31]

What Shepard had in common with Milne was that they were both geniuses in their own field, the former at drawing, the latter at creative writing. They also both had caring and supportive parents, a keen sense of the humorous and of the absurd, a love of cricket, and an association with *Punch* magazine. And most importantly, bearing in mind the project on which they were soon to collaborate, Shepard's son Graham and Milne's son Christopher each possessed a teddy bear!

Finally, both men had seen active service during the First World War.

Chapter 22

E. H. Shepard and the First World War (1914-1918)

The First World War commenced on 28 July 1914, by which time:

'Shepard had established a solid reputation as an artist and illustrator, managed to bring in a regular (if not large) income and the family had been able to move to a larger cottage in the village. Always keen on military matters, he chafed at not being allowed to volunteer to fight (He was both married and too old for the volunteer army) until 1915, when the rules relaxed and he signed up as an officer in the Royal Garrison Artillery.[1]

On 14 December 1914, Shepard, now aged 35, was commissioned as a second lieutenant in the Royal Artillery. The following month, he was assigned to the 105th Siege Battery which crossed to France in May 1916 and went into action at the Battle of the Somme.

By autumn 1916, Shepard had begun working for the Intelligence Department, sketching the combat area within sight of his battery position:

'On 16 February 1917, he was made an acting captain whilst second-in-command of his battery, and briefly served as an acting major in late April and early May of that year, during the Battle of Arras, before reverting to acting captain. He was promoted to substantive lieutenant on 1 July 1917. Whilst acting as captain, he was awarded the Military Cross [MC].' Shepard's citation reads as follows:

'For conspicuous gallantry and devotion to duty. As forward observation officer he continued to observe and send back valuable information, in spite of heavy shell and machine gun fire. His courage and coolness were conspicuous.'

'Late in 1917, 105th Siege Battery participated in the final stages of the Battle of Passchendaele where it came under heavy fire and suffered a number of casualties. At the end of the year, it was sent to help retrieve a disastrous situation on the Italian front, travelling by rail via Verona before coming into action on the Montello Hill.'

In April 1918, Shepard was invested with his MC by King George V at Buckingham Palace. He returned to Italy in time for the victory at Vittorio Veneto. After the Armistice of Villa Giusti in November 1918, Shepard was promoted to acting major in command of the battery and given the duty of administering captured enemy guns. Demobilisation began at Christmas 1918 and the 105th Siege Battery was disbanded in March 1919.[2]

Although Shepard served in the Royal Garrison Artillery, where the British field guns were located well to the rear of the trenches, part of his time was spent in the front line ('firing') trenches, so he was in no way immune from witnessing the horrors of war and the carnage of the battlefield.

For example, just like A. A. Milne, Shepard's duties included venturing out into no-man's-land after dark in order to repair the telephone lines which had been cut in many places by enemy shellfire.[3] In a letter written from Bronfay Farm, Bray-sur-Somme on 13 July 1916 during the Battle of the Somme, he recorded seeing a 'pretty large' number of casualties passing by on the way back from the front to the 'big advance dressing station a few hundred yards along the road'.[4] A battlefield drawing depicts buildings reduced to rubble around Zillebeke, in Belgium, with the bodies of soldiers who had been killed in action in the foreground.

Throughout the war, Shepard continued to contribute to *Punch*. Also, he wrote letters home, made numerous sketches and took photographs where possible.

Chapter 23

Shepard's brother Cyril and the Folly of War

Shepard's brother, Cyril Harry Shepard, joined the 9th Battalion, Devonshire Regiment as Second Lieutenant and was killed in action on 1 July 1916 on the first day of the battle of the Somme. He was aged 39. The circumstances of his death were as follows:

The 8th and 9th Battalions of the Devonshire Regiment, which were part of the 7th Division, attacked on 1 July 1916 from a point on the south-west side of Albert-Maricourt road due south of Mametz village, by a plantation called Mansel Copse.[1]

'Having been briefed on his Company's part in the coming attack near Mametz', Captain Duncan Lenox

Martin 'went on leave and built a model of the terrain over which the 9th Battalion would attack. Martin became convinced that, unless it was destroyed in the barrage, a particular German machine gun at Shrine Alley would catch his Company as it advanced along the Mansel Copse track'. In other words, his Company would be caught in the crossfire. 'He even pointed out to his brother officers where he and his men would fall.'

'At 07.27 hours on 1 July the first line of the 9th Devons advanced, under cover of fire from sixteen Stokes mortars, towards Mametz. Martin's fears were realised. As Duncan's No. 1 Company topped the rise and moved downhill past Mansel Copse, the machine gun 400 yards away in Shrine Alley mowed them down. Thirty-year-old Duncan Martin was one of the first to fall. That day the 9th Devons lost 141 killed, 268 wounded and 55 missing – a total of 464 casualties, amounting to 60% of their strength.

Their sister battalion, the 8th Devons, who were supporting them in the attack, lost another 207.'

Three days later the Reverend Ernest Crosse DSO MC, the 8th Devons' padre officiated at the burial of 160 men of the two battalions, including Captain Martin and Acting Lieutenant Cyril Shepard. The burials took place in a section of trench near a small wood called Mametz Copse.

Above the grave, since known as 'The Devonshire Cemetery', a wooden board was placed, inscribed with the words:

> The Devonshires held this trench.
> The Devonshires hold it still.[2]

'Some days after the battle Ernest found his brother's grave, remarking in his diary that he was grateful to feel so near to Cyril. He returned several times, telling his wife, Florence, that "it's such a strange feeling, I feel as if the place were a kind of home, and I feel we're kind of greeting each other. I always dream of after the war when you and I can go there together and I expect Rosemary [Cyril's widow] & Ethel [Cyril and Ernest's sister] will come too". So as not to lose the place, he marked up a trench map with the reference F17 a.9.6. putting a tiny cross on the precise spot.'[3]

Subsequently, for many years, Shepard returned to his brother's grave. He demonstrated his love for his late brother by sending drawings of the grave 'home to Cyril's widow and to their sister, Ethel.'[4]

Did Shepard, like Milne, suffer from shell shock, either during or after the First World War? Not ostensibly, but probably deep down, to a degree, as few if any who had witnessed such horrors escaped mentally unscathed.

Chapter 24

E. V. Lucas and the First World War

E. V. Lucas, who had been instrumental in bringing Shepard, the illustrator of Winnie-the-Pooh books and their author, Milne, together, explained that he was too old to fight in the First World War. When the war broke out, Lucas was aged 46. He said, he was 'not robust or athletic enough to falsify my age with any benefit to the army'.[1]

'Naturally the war directed most of the literary activities of us all. I could not fight, but there was nothing to stop me criticizing the foe. I began, immediately after the invasion of Belgium and the destruction of the library at Louvain, by compiling, in a fever of indignation, an anthology in praise of honest fighting. The full title was *Remember Louvain! A Little Book of Liberty and War*, and it included poems by Shakespeare, Wordsworth, Newbolt, and Kipling.

'A month or so later I was busy on a new version of *Struwwelpeter*, or *Shock-headed Peter*, the German nursery classic to which I gave an anti-Kaiser turn by calling it Swollen-headed William, with [cartoonist and illustrator] George Morrow to adapt the Pictures.'[2]

'In July 1916 my brother Perceval, who, though thirty-six when the trouble began, had enlisted at once, was killed in our Somme offensive, at Fricourt, leaving a widow (née Madeline Meynell) and three small daughters.'[3]

Chapter 25

E. H. Shepard and the Lost Wartime Sketches

In an article entitled 'First World War Sketches by Winnie-the-Pooh Illustrator Discovered in Trunk', published in *The London Telegraph* in 2016, Camilla Turner stated as follows:

'Now it has emerged that before he found fame as
A. A. Milne's illustrator, Ernest Shepard used his artistic talent to document his time in the trenches during the First World War through a series of humorous caricatures. The lost sketches, which were discovered in a trunk that lay untouched for 100 years, depict his experiences in some of the bloodiest battles on the Western Front as a captain in the Royal Garrison Artillery. Many sketches of life in the trenches show Shepard's upbeat humour, poking fun not only at his enemies but also at the pompousness of his commanders and the other

'Tommies' [British private soldiers]. However, as the war dragged on some drawings take on a more serious tone.'

'It was feared that Shepard's original wartime sketches had been lost when archivists at the Shepard Trust, custodians of his work, could not find any from that era.'

'However, researchers eventually found the trunk which Shepard had filled with all his WWI mementoes including unpublished drawings, watercolours and preparatory sketches. The box, untouched since Shepard's return to England in 1919, also contained his personal belongings and included his artist's tools and [military] uniform.'

James Campbell, who married Shepard's great-granddaughter, shed further light on the discovery:

'Mr Campbell, from Long Wittenham near Abingdon, Oxfordshire, said that he was approached by researchers who wanted use some of Shepard's sketches of the trenches for the centenary of the First World War. "To our astonishment we found that we didn't seem to have anything from his time in the trenches whatsoever, which was very odd", he said. "Then we found in our own private archive a large box which appeared not to have been opened in almost 100 years. Inside it was the most incredible material from the First World War - not only did it contain all his illustrations, cartoons, and paintings, but also his uniform, his briefcase, his pocketbook and his artist's material.'[1]

In his wartime cartoons, rendered in both pencil and watercolour, Shepard lampooned the enemy, for example by showing German soldiers using their grossly obese colleagues as springboards in order to vault Belgian trenches! He also caricatured his fellow officers of the 105th Siege Battery.

This included Captain M. G. Herbert, whom he portrayed booted and spurred with a tin helmet and a dandified costume, or at another time in the guise of a mad musical conductor![2]

However, there was a serious side to his work, where he showed British Tommies hunkered down in their trench, as well as his dugout (trench that is dug and roofed over as a shelter for troops[3]).

Shepard's skills as an illustrator were put to good use by the army. For instance, he made 'many tactical drawings showing topography, enemy positions, and distances'. In other words, identifying targets and assessing the range of the guns. On the technical side, he created images of British artillery pieces and made detailed drawings to illustrate the inner workings of artillery shells and their firing mechanisms.[4]

Corcoran said, 'One of the striking things about Shepard's drawings was that he was able to find humour in even the most grim of situations', for instance, British soldiers expelling a herd of cows from their barracks!

Corcoran continued, 'He obviously took a pop at the Germans but also sends up everyone else too including the British commanders for their pompousness as well as the standard Tommies, the Irish and the Italians.'[5]

At other times Shepard recorded events as they occurred: a crashed French biplane which had nosedived into the ground, a British tank on the move; artillery shells exploding in no man's land with plumes of white smoke and churned-up earth portrayed in watercolour; a battle at the Somme in 1916 involving aircraft, tanks, and infantry.

Perhaps most poignant of all are Shepard's battlefield scenes; one, for example, entitled 'Complete Desolation', captures the shell-ravaged landscape of the Somme, in black and white.

Chapter 26

'Pooh' and 'Christopher Robin' Make Their Debut

A forbear of Pooh, please excuse the pun, appeared in Milne's poem 'Teddy Bear', which was published in *Punch* on 13 February 1924:

'A bear, however hard he tries,
Grows tubby without exercise.
Our Teddy Bear is short and fat,
Which is not to be wondered at;
He gets what exercise he can
By falling off the ottoman,
But generally seems to lack
The energy to clamber back.'

By verse 11, 'Teddy Bear' has become 'Mr Edward Bear'.[1] This poem subsequently appeared in *When We Were Very Young* (published on 6 November of that same year).

In his Introduction to *When We Were Very Young*, Milne mentioned both Pooh and Christopher Robin by name. And Christopher Robin features in the second poem of the anthology, *Buckingham Palace*. In his introduction to *Now We Are Six* (published in 1927), both Pooh and 'his friend Piglet' are mentioned by Milne.

The name 'Winnie-the-Pooh' first appeared in Milne's 'Winnie-the-Pooh and the Wrong Bees', a Christmas story commissioned and published by the *Evening News*, a London newspaper, on 24 December 1925:[2]

'Here is Edward Bear, coming downstairs now, bump, bump, bump, on the back of his head, behind Christopher Robin. It is, as far as he knows, the only way of coming downstairs, but sometimes he feels that there really is another way, if only he could stop bumping for a moment and think of it. And then he feels that perhaps there isn't.

Anyhow, here he is at the bottom, and ready to be introduced to you. Winnie-the-Pooh.'

The story subsequently appeared in book form in the following year, 1926. But why 'Winnie'?

The story began in Canada, and it was Frederick Colebourn, son of Harry Colebourn, who provided the details, in a 'Biographical Sketch' of his father.

Harry Colebourn was born on 12 April 1887 in Birmingham, Warwickshire, UK. His father John was a domestic coachman, married to Alice. Frederick said: Harry

'came to Canada in 1905 when he was 18 years of age. He settled in Toronto initially and, in order to finance his university education, he worked in menial jobs such as selling fruit from door to door on the streets in Toronto and as a deckhand on commercial vessels plying the Great Lakes.'

'In 1908, he enrolled at the Ontario Veterinary College located in Guelph [south-western Ontario]. On 25 April 1912, he received his degree as a Veterinary Surgeon and following his graduation, he returned to Dewsbury, England to re-unite with his family.'

'Following a short stay, he returned to Canada. On 3 July 1912, he accepted a veterinary appointment with the Department of Agriculture, Health of Animals Branch in Winnipeg [province of Ontario]. In the same year he joined the l8th Mounted Rifles as a militia officer and then was seconded to the 34th Regiment of Cavalry, Fort Garry Horse on 15 May 1912.'

When the First World War broke out, said Frederick, Harry:

'was already a trained officer and immediately offered his services to his country.

Subsequently, he was given leave of absence from the Department of Agriculture and left Winnipeg on 23 August 19l4, bound for Valcartier, Quebec. While en route to Valcartier, he was attached to both the Fort Garry Horse and the Canadian Army Veterinary Corps (CAVC).'

Now came the crucial event in the life, not only of Harry, but also of a small furry creature!

'On 24 August, the train stopped at White River [Township in Northern Ontario] where father purchased a small, black, female cub bear for the sum of $20.00 from a hunter who had killed her mother. Shortly after this, father named his little cub, "Winnie" after the City of Winnipeg, his home town.' On 12 September 1914, Harry:

'was Taken On Strength of [i.e., joined] the Second Canadian Infantry Brigade Headquarters under the command of Lieutenant Colonel Arthur W. Currie, who was later on to become Canada's leading general of the Canadian Expeditionary Force.'

In his father's diaries, said Frederick, Harry recorded that:

'On 3 October 1914, he and "Winnie" embarked from Gase Bay [sic Gaspé Bay, south-eastern Quebec] en route for England aboard the SS Manitou along with four other liners heading for England. On 17 October they disembarked and left Devonport [naval dockyard, Devon], England, for Salisbury Plain [British military training area in Wiltshire] at 7:00 p.m. that morning. "Winnie" was to remain with him and a pet to the Second Canadian Infantry Brigade Headquarters while he remained in England.'

'"Winnie" quickly became a pet to many of the soldiers and would follow them around like a tame dog in their off-duty hours at Salisbury Plain. There were numerous photos taken of her with the men and these photos often became a keepsake for them to treasure.'

Harry was informed that "Winnie" would not be permitted to travel with the Canadian military to the battlefields of France, 'consequently', said Frederick:

'On 9 December 1914, father proceeded to the London Zoo with his "pet" where he left her in safe keeping until the end of the war. According to his diary, it was his full intention to bring "Winnie" back to Canada with him after the war was over. His diaries indicated that he was very fond of her and would often visit her when on leave from war zones in France.'

'However, when the war ended in 1918', said Frederick, his father 'reversed his original intentions to bring "Winnie" home to Winnipeg and, instead, donated her to the London Zoo as a gesture of his appreciation for the London Zoo's efforts in caring for her during those four war years.'

'It was to be noted that "Winnie" had also become a feature attraction for the many thousands of visitors and especially young children. She was considered to be completely trustworthy by her bear keepers who said that of all the bears they had in the Zoo, "Winnie" was the only one they could say this about. She was also the tamest and best-behaved bear that the Zoo ever had.'

Most significantly, said Frederick:

'Two of her admirers of that early period after the war were A. A. Milne, a writer, and his young son Christopher Robin. They frequently visited the zoo where the young Milne boy would always want to go and see "Winnie".'[3]

At London Zoo, 'Winnie':

'was much loved for her playfulness and gentleness. Zoo keeper Ernest Scales stated that Winnie was "the only bear they ever trusted entirely", letting children, like Christopher Robin, go right inside her enclosure and even ride on her back.'[4] In fact, photographs exist of Christopher standing inside Winnie's enclosure, offering snacks to the bear as her keeper looked on!

Milne and Christopher would doubtless have been aware of the story of the bear cub 'Winnie', and of how her father had been killed by a senseless act of cruelty in a distant land, more than three-thousand miles away.

Chapter 27

Enter E. H. Shepard, and 'Pooh' and 'Christopher Robin' Come to Life!

How did Shepard go about creating the fifty or so drawings to be included in *When We Were Very Young*? Authors James Campbell, and Minette Shepard, E. H. Shepard's granddaughter through his son Graham, said:

'We know that he drew and sketched incessantly, and he himself regularly remarked that there was rarely a day when he did not draw something of interest. He generally carried a small sketchbook and pencil with him in order to quickly record things he found of interest, and a number of these small sketchbooks still exist, attesting to Shepard's ability to capture a scene with just a few lines. He would often then use these quick sketches to work up more detailed drawings in larger drawing books.'[1]

When it came to creating a likeness of Pooh:

'To start with, Shepard drew Christopher Robin's own teddy bear, but both he and Milne agreed that this was not going to work. The bear was too angular and had a rather firm jaw. They needed a bear that was less threatening, more cuddly and with a twinkle in his eye. So Shepard returned to his own children's toybox, and to Growler, his son Graham's teddy bear. Writing about this time, Shepard said, "My son, Graham, had a teddy to which he had been deeply attached as a child and I used this bear as my model".'[2]

As for depicting the owner of Pooh, said Shepard:

'I also had a number of drawings I had made of Graham as a boy of six and these were very useful when, later on, I came to draw Christopher Robin.'[3]

Christopher himself stated that:

'If Christopher Robin seems a rather odd little boy, in one respect he is now less odd than he once was. Today his long hair and curious clothes are very much in fashion. But at the time, when other little boys had short hair, shirts and ties, they were decidedly unusual. Was this Shepard's idea, or my father's - or whose?'

'First let me say that it had nothing to do with Shepard. It is true that he used his imagination when he drew the animals, but me he drew from life. I did indeed look just like that.'[4]

According to Shepard, his son Graham played a part when it came to the depiction of Christopher Robin.

So appreciative was Milne of Shepard that in the Introduction to *When We Were Very Young*, he mentioned Shepard specifically by name:

'You may wonder sometimes who is supposed to be saying the verses. Is it the Author, that strange but uninteresting person, or is it Christopher Robin, or some other boy or girl, or Nurse, or Hoo? If you are not quite sure, then it is probably Hoo. I don't know if you have ever met Hoo, but he is one of those curious children who look four on Monday, and eight on Tuesday, and are really twenty-eight on Saturday. He had a great deal to do with these verses. In fact, you might almost say that this book is entirely the unaided work of Christopher Robin, Hoo, and Mr Shepard, who drew the pictures.'[5]
'Hoo' therefore appears to be a part of Milne's imagination!

Finally Milne, in a copy of *Winnie-the-Pooh* that he presented to Shepard, inscribed the words:

> When I am gone
> Let Shepard decorate my tomb,
> And put (if there is room)
> Two pictures on the stone;
> Piglet from page a hundred and eleven

And Pooh and Piglet walking (157).
And [Saint] Peter, thinking that they are my own,
Will welcome me to heaven.

Milne's son Christopher was equally unstinting in his praise of Shepard. He said:

'Pooh, who had been developing under my father's pen, began to develop under Shepard's pen as well. What is it that gives Pooh his particularly Poohish look? It is the position of his eye. The eye that starts as quite an elaborate affair, level with the top of Pooh's nose, gradually moves downwards and ends up a mere dot level with his mouth. And in this dot the whole of Pooh's character can be read.'[6]

Chapter 28

The Characters and Their Locations

Christopher gave a wonderfully descriptive account of how the fictional locations of the Pooh stories corresponded, in many instances, to the real-life topography of the environs of Cotchford Farm:

'There is a path through Posingford Wood - Nanny and I soon found it - that takes you up to the Forest.'[1] This was Ashdown Forest, covering an area of about 10 square miles of East Sussex. 'Pooh's Forest and Ashdown Forest are identical.'[2]

'At the very top of the Forest is Gill's Lap' continued Christopher, which he could see from the window of his nursery:

'You could see Gill's Lap from a great many places for miles around - a clump of pines on the top of a hill. And, of course you can see it as Shepard drew it in *The House at Pooh Corner*. In the book, it is Galleon's Lap, but otherwise it is exactly as described, an enchanted spot before ever Pooh came along to add to its magic.'[3]

As for the 'Hundred Acre Wood' of the stories, this was 'really the Five Hundred Acre Wood' in Ashdown Forest, East Sussex. It was 'very different from Posingford Wood. 'It is a real forest with giant beech trees, all dark and mysterious.'[4]

In the Five Hundred Acre Wood there was a tree which he was 'particularly fond of', said Christopher:

'It was only just inside the wood and the path ran right by it. So, Nanny and I must have discovered it on our first visit. It was a huge and ancient beech tree, one of a group of about half a dozen. It looked as if over the centuries it had grown tired of holding its arms up to the sky and had allowed its lower branches to droop. One branch in particular came out horizontally then curved downwards to rest its elbow on the ground.'

'And at this point you could sit on it. Or you could stand on it and walk a little way along it and then jump off into the soft carpet of dead leaves spread out below. You could practise balancing, then practise jumping. It was difficult to walk very far for the branch was moss covered and slippery and soon got too steep, and there was nothing to hold on to. So then you could sit astride it and wriggle your way forward.'[5]

'Posingford, the Forest, the Five Hundred Acre [Wood]: this was where it all happened', said Christopher:

'but not where it started. It started much nearer home: at the top of the garden, in an ancient walnut tree. The tree was hollow inside and a great gash in its trunk had opened up to make a door. It was the perfect tree house for a five-year-old. I could climb inside and sit on the soft, crumbly floor. In the walls were cracks and ledges where things could be put; and high above my head was a green and blue ceiling of leaves and sky. Pooh and I claimed it. It was Pooh's House, really, but there was plenty of room for us both inside, and here we came to play our small, quiet happy games together.'

'I must now introduce the toys. Pooh was the oldest, only a year younger than I was [i.e., a first birthday present], and my inseparable companion. As you find us in the poem '*Us Two*', so we were in real life.'

> 'Us Two'
> 'Wherever I am, there's always Pooh,
> There's always Pooh and Me.
> Whatever I do, he wants to do,
> "Where are you going today?" says Pooh:
> "Well, that's very odd 'cos I was too.
> Let's go together", says Pooh, says he.
> "Let's go together", says Pooh.'

Here, Milne is alluding to that precious human commodity, companionship, the kind he no doubt enjoyed with his son.

'Every child has his favourite toy, and every only-child has a special need for one. Pooh was mine, and probably, clasped in my arms, not really very different from the countless other bears clasped in the arms of countless other children. From time to time he went to the cleaners, and from time to time ears had to be sewn on again, lost eyes replaced and paws renewed.' Nanny Brockwell presumably did the honours in this respect!

'Eeyore, too, was an early present. Perhaps in his younger days he had held his head higher, but by the time the stories came to be written his neck had gone like that and this had given him his gloomy disposition.'

In fact, the Milnes did own a real live donkey. She was called 'Jessica' but, said Christopher, she had:

'no connection whatever with Eeyore, except that she lived in a field a little like Eeyore's. It was Nanny's job, helped by Tasker and slightly helped by me, to catch her and saddle her.

Sometimes this was easy, sometimes not. Our first outing was a cautious trip up the lane where, with luck, nothing too disastrous could happen.'

'And I can still recall the horrifying moment when Jessica stopped and her legs began to sag. I was snatched from her back and Nanny and I watched, appalled, as she crumpled up on the ground, then rolled on to her side, then on to her back, then kicked up her legs in the air and let out an ear-splitting bellow, then rolled - still bellowing - from side to side, then scrambled to her feet and waited for me to remount. But Nanny said: "I don't think you'd better, dear". And I didn't think I'd better, either. And we all three walked home.'

'On subsequent trips we knew what to expect, that it was just one of the things Jessica liked doing, and so, when her legs started sagging, I got off and waited until it was all over.'[6]

'Piglet was a present from a neighbour who lived over the way, a present for the small boy she so often used to meet out walking with his Nanny.'

These were the three main characters around which the stories revolved, said Christopher, but more were required and so:

'two were invented: Owl and Rabbit. Owl was owlish from the start and always remained so. But Rabbit, I suspect, began by being just the owner of the hole in which Pooh got stuck and then, as the stories went on, became less rabbity and more Rabbity; for rabbits are not by nature good organizers.'

'Both Kanga and Tigger were later arrivals, presents from my parents, carefully chosen, not just for the delight they might give to their new owner, but also for their literary possibilities. So, there they were, and to a certain extent their characters were theirs from birth. As my father said, making it all sound very simple, you only had to look at them to see at once that

Eeyore was gloomy, Piglet squeaky, Tigger bouncy and so on.'[7]

Christopher now explained how his handful of inanimate toys became the characters of which the Pooh stories were composed.

'The bear took his place in the nursery and gradually he began to come to life. It started in the nursery; it started with me. It could really start nowhere else, for the toys lived in the nursery and they were mine and I played with them. And as I played with them and talked to them and gave them voices to answer with, so they began to breathe. But alone I couldn't take them very far. I needed help.'

'So my mother joined me and she and I and the toys played together, and gradually more life, more character flowed into them, until they reached a point at which my father could take over. Then, as the first stories were written, the cycle was repeated. The Pooh in my arms, the Pooh sitting opposite me at the breakfast table, was a Pooh who had climbed trees in search of honey, who had got stuck in a rabbit hole, who was "a bear of no brain at all".'[8]

Shepard shed further light on the origins of Pooh:

'I had a perfect model for him in my son's Teddy. Where he came from I do not know but he had the comfortable air and the right waist measurement for Milne's leading character.[9] He was a wonderful bear, quite the best fellow I have seen anywhere, and he seemed to have a character of his own.'[10] Not only that, said Shepard, but:

'Milne and I went over the ground close by his home at Hartfield and he showed me the various spots that formed the background for his characters. So that I was able to draw many of the places with the comfortable feeling that "it really happened here". The work was sheer joy for me, more especially as Milne gave me a free hand and had shown such confidence in me from the start.'[11]

In fact, as already mentioned, Milne had been unsure about Shepard's suitability as an illustrator of his 'Pooh' books, until he saw the light!

To the person who reads one of Milne's 'Pooh' books for the very first time, the poems in the first two volumes and the short stories in the second two volumes come as a delight. However, when combined with Shepard's exquisite drawings, the works are converted into an art form, once seen, never forgotten!

The first mention of a bear comes in the poem '*Lines and Squares*' in the first book, *When We Were Very Young*. But this is clearly about a real bear in a zoo, who bears (again, please excuse the pun) no relation to Pooh!

Shepard's first drawing of a bear which looks like Pooh, though Milne does not mention her by name (and it is a 'her', because the 'Winnie' after which she was named was a female cub), comes in the same volume, in the poem

'*Halfway Down*'. Here, the bear is lying at the top of the stairs and a little boy, her owner, is sitting on a step below. A few pages later, in the poem '*Teddy Bear*', the toy that became Pooh is even more recognisable, being somewhat rotund in shape!

In the second volume of poetry, *Now We Are Six*, in a postscript to the introduction, Milne mentions the name of both Pooh and Piglet for the first time. And it is in the poem '*Sneezles*', that the name Christopher Robin first appears:

'*Sneezles*'

'Christopher Robin
Had wheezles
And sneezles,
They bundled him
Into
His bed.
They gave him what goes
With a cold in the nose,
And some more for a cold
In the head.'

A few poems later, in 'Us Two', Pooh, and a little boy who, from Shepard's depiction, is undoubtedly Christopher Robin, appear together for the first time.

Subsequently, in the poem '*The Engineer*', Pooh and nearly all of his friends appear as depicted by Shepard, including Eeyore, Piglet, Kanga and Roo, and of course, Christopher Robin!

In the Introduction to *Now We Are Six*, Milne said:

'We want you to know that the name of the book doesn't mean that this is us being six all the time, but that it is about as far as we've got at present, and we half think of stopping there.'

Bearing in mind that the book was published in 1927 and that Milne had seen active service in the First World War with all its horrors and loss of life, this suggestion by him that he half wished that his life had been frozen in childhood is hardly surprising! There are echoes of this, of course, in J. M. Barrie's eponymously-named fictional character '*Peter Pan: The Boy Who Never Grew Up*'.

Finally, in the third and fourth Pooh books, *Winnie-the-Pooh* and *The House at Pooh Corner*, Milne and Shepard absolutely let rip, as Pooh, Christopher Robin, and all their friends have adventures galore!

'Rabbit's clever', said Pooh thoughtfully.
'Yes', said Piglet, 'Rabbit's clever.'
'And he has Brain.'
'Yes', said Piglet, 'Rabbit has Brain.'
There was a long silence.
'I suppose', said Pooh, 'that that's why he never understands anything.'

'Pooh, when I'm - you know - when I'm not doing Nothing, will you come up here sometimes?'
'Just Me?'
'Yes, Pooh.'
'Will you be here too?'
'Yes, Pooh, I will be really. I promise I will be, Pooh.'
'That's good', said Pooh.
'Pooh, promise you won't forget about me, ever. Not even when I'm a hundred.'
Pooh thought for a little.
'How old shall I be then?'
'Ninety-nine.'
Pooh nodded.
'I promise', he said.
Still with his eyes on the world Christopher Robin put out a hand and felt for Pooh's paw.
'Pooh', said Christopher Robin earnestly, if I - if I'm not quite – ' he stopped and tried again –'Pooh, *whatever* happens, you will understand, won't you?'
'Understand what?'
'Oh, nothing.' He laughed and jumped to his feet.
'Come on!'
'Where?' said Pooh.
'Anywhere', said Christopher Robin.

Does this not reflect one of the most profound wishes of any human being – the earnest wish not to be forgotten? And was there ever an author like Milne, who, in his 'Pooh' books, combined such wit and gaiety on the one hand with such pathos on the other? Those who have lost loved ones may find Christopher Robin's expression of his desire always to be remembered almost unbearable because yes, here Milne is alluding to companionship, and to that most precious of all human commodities, love.

Chapter 29

Success, But at What Cost?

Christopher Milne's *The Enchanted Places* was published in 1974 by Methuen. In it he gave full vent to his annoyance at the way his father's creation, 'Winnie-the-Pooh' had ruined his life.

'If I had been a different sort of person there might well have been no problem', he said, but:

'Unfortunately, the fictional Christopher Robin refused to die, and he and his real-life namesake were not always on the best of terms. Actually, it was not one but two problems. First: Christopher Robin and the Schoolboy [i.e., as a youth]; secondly: Christopher Robin and the Man [i.e., as a grown-up]. The two are separated not just in time but by the fact that two quite different sides of my personality were the cause.'

'Take the Schoolboy first. This was by far the lesser of the two. It was a problem caused by my shyness.' Christopher now described how his life had been made miserable by being bullied at school, on account of his father's 'Winnie-the- Pooh' books:

'Christopher Robin was beginning to be what he was later to become: a sore place that looked as if it would never heal up. I vividly recall how intensely painful it was to me to sit in my study at Stowe [School] while my neighbours played the famous - and now cursed - gramophone record remorselessly over and over again.' This was a reference to a set of three records of poems from *When We Were Very Young* by Milne, set to music and sung by US singer Frank Luther.

'Eventually, the joke, if not the record, wore out. They handed it to me, and I took it and broke it into a hundred fragments and scattered them over a distant field. But mostly I had other things to think about and didn't bother about being Christopher Robin one way or the other. And because I spent so much time at school not bothering and the entire holidays not bothering, it never occurred to me that perhaps I ought to be blaming somebody for it all. In fact I blamed nobody. I felt no resentment. My relations with my father were quite unaffected.'[1]

'Christopher Robin and the Man is a less happy story. Here the cause of the trouble was jealousy.' He and his father 'had been companions, but now our ways were to part.

Admittedly fortune had then smiled on him.' However:

'fortune was now frowning on me. I was the wrong person in the wrong place with qualifications nobody wanted. But this didn't alter the fact that he had pressed on to become a famous writer and here was I staring up at him, filled with resentment. Other fathers were reaching down helping hands to their sons. But what was mine doing? What, to be fair, could mine do? He had made his own way by his own efforts and he had left behind him no path that could be followed. But were they entirely his own efforts? Hadn't I come into it somewhere?'

'In pessimistic moments, when I was trudging London in search of an employer wanting to make use of such talents as I could offer, it seemed to me, almost, that my father had got to where he was by climbing upon my infant shoulders, that he had filched from me my good name and had left me with nothing but the empty fame of being his son.'

'That is how I saw it, looking up at him. How did he see it, looking down at me? Neither of us knew what the other thought. We could only guess. Did he guess right? Did he sympathize? Was he resentful? Did he have any feelings of guilt?

Well, he had his own battles to fight and, curiously, they were not dissimilar from mine. If I was jealous of him, he was no less jealous of himself. If I wanted to escape from Christopher Robin, so, too, did he.'[2]

On 24 July 1948, Christopher married his first cousin, Lesley de Sélincourt, daughter of his mother Daphne's younger brother Aubrey and his wife Irene. There was friction in the family, however, and Milne's wife Daphne had not spoken to her younger brother Aubrey 'for twenty-five years or so, since the row over borrowed money that had never been returned'.[3]

Aubrey de Sélincourt was a war hero, who had served with the North Staffordshire Regiment at Gallipoli and subsequently with 25 Squadron, Royal Flying Corps. On 28 May 1917, he was shot down but survived and remained a prisoner for the rest of the war. Aubrey became a distinguished writer, classical scholar, translator, and headmaster of Clayesmore (public) School in Dorset. In 1919, he married the poet Irene Rutherford McLeod. On 6 May 1925, their daughter Lesley was born.

Apart from the longstanding antipathy between Daphne and Aubrey, Christopher's parents were allegedly horrified at the prospect of him marrying his first cousin, perhaps because of the biological danger to any resultant offspring. If so, their fears were entirely justified, as will be seen.

Daphne's feelings towards her son became increasingly bitter, so much so that she 'gave instructions that a sculpture of Christopher's head' was to be buried under the trees where her dog had been buried, 'where she would never see it again'.[4]

Meanwhile, in his search for employment, said Christopher:

'I was answering advertisements and being interviewed with total lack of success. Indeed, my search at one point took me – unwittingly - to the very brink of that path that so many once proud ex-army officers had followed on [their] sad journey from hope to despair'.[5] In other words, he had contemplated suicide. 'Well, if nobody wanted me, if nobody was looking for a very shy young man who had once been quite good at solving differential equations, who knew how to build a Bailey Bridge [portable prefabricated bridge developed by the British during the Second World War] and defuse a Teller mine [German made anti-tank mine], who had scraped a third-class Honours Degree in English Literature, and who was handy with a tenon saw, if nobody would employ me, I must employ myself. I toyed with the idea of making furniture. In the end I decided to sell books. For here was something my wife and I could do together as partners; here was something we could do in a part of England of our own choosing; and if I wasn't too happy about four of the books [i.e., the 'Pooh' volumes'], there were still plenty of others.'[6]

'However hard I tried to play down Christopher Robin, however little space I allowed on my shelves to the Pooh books, people would inevitably think of mine as "The Christopher Robin Bookshop". However much I wanted to succeed as a bookseller on my own merits, people would inevitably conclude that I was succeeding partly at least on my father's reputation. They might even think (wrongly) that my father's money was subsidizing the venture.'[7]

'There were two things that were then overshadowing my life and that I needed to escape from: my father's fame and "Christopher Robin".

Yet, here I was apparently deliberately seeking out his shadow so as to work beneath it, choosing a trade that would put me on public exhibition as Christopher Robin, wrapping up the books he had written. Was it that I was deliberately turning to face the dragon that had been pursuing me? I must be honest and confess no such courageous intention. I was running away, all right. I was running away from London.'

'London was the scene of my father's successes. London was the scene of my failures. Neither Lesley nor I had any love for the place, and every weekend we used to escape into the country. What was there to keep us here? Why should we not make our escape permanent!'[8]

In 1951 Christopher and Lesley relocated to the West Country, to Dartmouth in Devonshire where they opened a bookshop. Christopher subsequently declared:

'Selfishly I was glad that I lived in Devon and had a bookshop that I could not easily leave.

Children drift away from their parents as they grow up, and it is right that they should. I had been very close to mine, especially to my father, for rather longer than is usual, and so the drifting when it came was perhaps a little farther than is usual.'[9]

In his autobiography, Christopher Milne had been open and honest about his feelings, vis-à-vis his father Alan and his father's 'Winnie-the-Pooh' books. However, as an adult, he had clearly developed a tremendous chip on his shoulder over the way his namesake, the fictional owner of 'Pooh Bear' had blighted his life, and much of his anger was directed against his father. But was Christopher justified?

When Milne began writing the first book to feature the bear that became Winnie-the-Pooh, namely *When We Were Very Young* (published in 1924) he could not possibly have imagined how successful this, and the three succeeding 'Pooh' volumes would be. In fact, they far eclipsed his other writings and his plays, which galled him because he considered himself primarily to be a playwright.

Milne's fourth and last 'Pooh book', *The House at Pooh Corner* was published in 1928, five years before Christopher commenced at Stowe School, where he was bullied unmercifully on this account. In the UK's public schools of the pre-war period, bullying was not only endemic but it was built into the system, in the form of 'fagging' whereby junior boys performed minor chores for senior pupils.

Had Christopher accepted the situation for what it was, acknowledged his father Alan's success for what it was without feeling jealous about it, and not behaved in a self-pitying and churlish manner, his adult life would undoubtedly have been a much happier one!

Another reason why the rift between Christopher and his parents was unlikely to heal was that his wife Lesley simply did not like them. Christopher told the broadcaster, writer, and former politician Gyles Brandreth that, 'Publicly he wasn't reconciled to his parents.' As for Brandreth, he stated that:

'Knowing her, I think that was in large part because of Lesley. She didn't like them. "They weren't likeable", she told me.'[10]

Christopher's attitude is in stark contrast with that of his father Alan, whose love for his son is reflected in the loving poems and stories that he wrote about the fictional Christopher Robin.

After the publication of the fourth 'Pooh' book, Milne and Shepard's literary agents and publishers, Curtis Brown, and Methuen and Dutton respectively, said James Campbell, were 'well aware of the potential financial rewards', that the publication of further 'Pooh books' would bring, and they were 'encouraging, at times pleading, for more books'. However, 'Milne was adamant; he already felt hemmed in by Pooh and distracted from what he saw as his "serious" work as a playwright and poet, and had no inclination to continue'.[11]

Chapter 30

From Milne's Perspective

In his book *By Way of Introduction*, published in 1929, Milne stated that he did not regret having given the fictional 'Christopher Robin' his son's name, and he explained why. It was because he regarded his son, and the fictional Christopher Robin as being two quite different entities.[1]

So who, in Milne's eyes, was the fictional Christopher Robin? Who was 'The hero now', he asked himself, 'of *When We Were Very Young*; soon to be the hero of *Winnie-the-Pooh* and two other books? To me he was, and remained, the child of my imagination. When I thought of him, I thought of him in the forest, living in his tree as no child really lives; not in the nursery, where a differently named child (so far as we in this house are concerned) was playing with his animals. For this reason, I have not felt self-conscious when writing about him, nor apologetic at the thought of exposing my own family to the public gaze.'

In respect of Pooh and his companions, said Milne, 'I have exploited them for my own profit'. However, he continued:

'I feel I have not exploited the legal
[real-life] Christopher Robin. All I have got from Christopher Robin is a name which he never uses, an introduction to his friends … and a gleam which I have tried to follow.'

Furthermore, Milne believed that 'the dividing line between the imaginary and the real Christopher Robin' became:

'fainter with each book. 'This, then, brings me (at last) to one of the reasons why these verses and stories have come to an end. I feel that the legal Christopher Robin has already had more publicity than I want for him. Moreover, since he is growing up, he will soon feel that he has had more publicity than he wants for himself. We all, young and old, hope to make some sort of a name, but we want to make it in our own chosen way, and, if possible, by our own exertions'.[2]

In other words, Milne was both concerned for and protective towards his son Christopher.

Chapter 31

Aftermath

A. A. Milne

Milne, said Campbell:

'had been hugely impressed and influenced' by writer Kenneth Grahame's children's book *The Wind in the Willows*, first published in 1908' and he 'had persuaded Grahame to allow him to dramatize the book into a stage play - eventually becoming *Toad of Toad Hall* - and he had been working on it, on and off [with Harold Fraser-Simson as composer of the music], throughout the 1920s. During this time, Milne became increasingly aware of how dissatisfied Grahame was with the various attempts to illustrate *The Wind in the Willows* and he persuaded Shepard, who had already illustrated Grahame's [two collections of childhood reminiscences] *The Golden Age* [1895] and *Dream Days* [1898], to approach Grahame – but this time with Milne's personal recommendation - to make a fresh attempt at capturing the essence of the animals of the riverbank and the wild wood.

Initially, Shepard was cautious, and Grahame was anxious, but the resulting illustrations were a triumph, both with Kenneth Grahame and the public, and have never since been out of print.'[1]

E. H. Shepard

In 1921 Shepard:

'was invited to join the *Punch* table - effectively the editorial board of the magazine - which met weekly for lunch around the table to determine both the content of the magazine and its editorial stance. Further, participants were invited to carve their names into the table itself, which was both an honour and a sign of acceptance into the *Punch* inner circle.'[2]

Because Shepard's wife Florence was suffering from severe asthma, the couple decided to relocate from Shamley Green to Long Meadow, a new house situated on the Downs near Guildford.

However:

'in September 1927, shortly before they were due to move in, Florence went into hospital in London for a minor and routine nasal operation to provide some relief from her asthma - and died under the anaesthetic.'[3]

Having seen her father safely ensconced at Long Meadow, his daughter Mary commenced studying at the Slade School of Fine Art in London. She subsequently became an artist and illustrator in her own right.[4]

By the summer of 1928, Shepard, 'was back at work on the Pooh illustrations'.[5] Campbell said:

'Shepard found himself increasingly busy as the 1930s progressed. Not only was he fulfilling additional work on Winnie-the-Pooh projects, but he was also working for *Punch* on a weekly basis and undertaking a wide range of commissions, many for book illustrations.'

'As Shepard took up the critical role of principal cartoonist for *Punch* in the mid-1930s, now responsible for the lead political cartoon each week, he became even busier. In this role, he contributed to the editorial stance of the magazine over a significant period that covered the rise of the Nazis in Germany, the abdication crisis of 1936, the appeasement movement and the Munich Agreement of 1938, the descent into war and the appointment of Winston Churchill as wartime prime minister.'[6]

In 1937, Shepard's daughter Mary married Edmund Knox, who had been editor of *Punch* since 1932 (and remained so until 1949) on the retirement of Owen Seaman. So, the family's connection with that magazine continued for another generation.

'As Shepard's reputation soared, he was obliged, due to pressure of work, to decline certain commissions, including one to illustrate Mary Poppins by P. L. Travers.' This was a collection of 8 children's books by Australian-British writer Pamela Lindon Travers. In the event, it was Shepard's daughter, Mary, 'a distinguished illustrator in her own right', who was awarded the commission and 'who went on to illustrate all of the Mary Poppins books from 1934 to 1988'![7]

Chapter 32

The Second World War (1939-1945)

A. A. Milne

According to Campbell:

'Milne continued to submit pieces for *Punch* through the 1930s and 1940s, but increasingly his light and frivolous style, which had so caught the public mood in the 1920s, failed to resonate as the reading public's taste moved on. Having had at one time four plays simultaneously running in the West End of London in the 1920s, Milne had none of his plays staged after the late 1930s; and although he continued to submit work to *Punch*, by the 1940s, E. V. Knox had to write to Milne to explain that while his writing was as good as it had ever been, the public was no longer receptive to his whimsical style and, with regret, *Punch* would no longer be able to publish Milne's contributions in the future. It was a difficult and sad end to a forty-year relationship.'[1] For Milne, this would have been a bitter pill to swallow!

E. H. Shepard

At the outbreak of the Second World War Shepherd:

'volunteered for the Local Defence Volunteers (the "Home Guard") at the earliest opportunity,[2] where he was actively involved in "C" Company, 4th (Guildford) Battalion, Surrey Home Guard. Shepard threw himself into this "war work" and was an active member of the unit, patrolling at night and weekends and drawing maps.'[3]

In October 1931, Shepard's son Graham married Ann Faith Gibbon who was British by birth but had been brought up in Canada. In 1937, their daughter Minette was born. Early in the Second World War Graham enlisted in the Royal Naval Volunteer Reserve. Meanwhile, Ann travelled to Montréal, Canada to be near to her family, taking Minette with her.[4]

On 21 September 1943 Graham lost his life when his Royal Naval corvette, HMS Polyanthus, was torpedoed and sunk in the North Atlantic.

On 18 November 1944 Shepard was re-married, to Norah Caroll, a nurse from St Mary's Hospital, Paddington.[5]

When the Second World War ended, Shepard's 'first peacetime commission was to illustrate *Jeremy* by novelist Hugh Walpole, then a highly popular author with substantial sales'.[6] Meanwhile, Minette returned to the UK with her mother Ann.

Christopher Milne

Christopher declared that, like his father, he was a pacifist.

'My father gave me reasons in a small book called *War Aims Unlimited*' (by Milne himself, published by Methuen in 1941).

'To put them very briefly, they were that Hitler was different: different from anything he had ever imagined possible; that terrible though the war was, peace under Hitler would have been even more terrible.'[7]

What finally persuaded Christopher to renounce his pacifism, he said, was the sound of German bombers flying in the sky above Cotchford 'on their leisurely way to bomb London'. Therefore, he said, 'I'm not going back to Cambridge [University] next year [1940]. I want to join the army'.[8]

Christopher spent 'about eight months in the LDV' (Home Guard)[9] prior to joining the Second Training Battalion of the Royal Engineers at Newark, Nottinghamshire.[10]

In Chapter 19 of his book *Beyond the World of Pooh* (2000), headed 'War - The Horror', Christopher described seeing the body of a fellow sapper named Pocket:

'A shell had landed just in front of him and blown him over, so that his head was broken and spilled like an egg that has been dropped on the floor.'[11]

Christopher also described being 'near a farmhouse that had suddenly come under very heavy mortar fire'.[12]

A sapper, which was Christopher's wartime occupation, is a soldier responsible for building and repairing roads and bridges and laying and clearing mines,[13] tasks which of course are fraught with extreme danger. In practice, said Christopher:

'when a storm was raging, the infantry could make a dash for it and risk getting wet. Tanks had their armour to keep them dry. But sappers worked in the open, slowly, carefully, often in quite large groups and with nothing to protect them. So when the storm broke, we took cover and waited until it was over. After all, the German guns only had a limited number of shells. Even if they could see us, they could never afford to fire at us all the time. There were other more important targets. But in bed at night, it was very different. Nights were usually quiet - but not quite always; and then the bed could be the most miserable of places, with nothing to distract one, nothing to do but lie awake and tremble, waiting wretchedly for the next explosion. And oh, how close and menacing they always seemed on these occasions. And so, I lay there waiting and waiting for the nightmare to come to an end.'[14]

Christopher described how he became the victim of an enemy shell, which:

'made, so it seemed to me, no sound but a puff, a sort of buffet somewhere behind my head. I scarcely heard it. I never saw it. And luckily, I never felt it. A few days later, my parents learned that I had been wounded and placed on the "seriously ill" list.'[15]

'I have often looked back on five years in the army', including 'my four years with the 56th Division' and 'my two and a half years in Italy' and:

'sometimes I have felt that they were five wasted years, years that could have been better spent qualifying for some profession, years that put me at a disadvantage compared with those who, younger than I, had missed the war and got ahead: sometimes I felt that I was one of war's casualties. But that mood passed. At other times I looked back with private pride and satisfaction on what I had done. It had not been much, really. But I was proud that I had started in the ranks, proud that I had spent so long overseas, proud to have been in the 56th, serving in Italy throughout the campaign, proud to have achieved my ambition of commanding a platoon in a divisional field company, and very, very proud that I had been wounded.'[16] In other words, Christopher wore his war wounds as a badge of honour.

Chapter 33

Clare Milne (born June 1956)

Christopher Milne prided himself on being financially independent and not benefiting in any way from royalties from his father's books, and the 'Pooh' books in particular. But all that was to change when, in June 1956, four months after the death of Milne on 31 January 1956, Christopher and Lesley's daughter Clare was born, with cerebral palsy, a condition marked by impaired muscle coordination, and/or other disabilities, caused by damage to the brain before or at birth.[1] Christopher said:

'Once we had accepted Clare's disability and its effect on us all, there were plenty of other things we could be happy about, plenty to enjoy, plenty to be grateful for. And at the top of the list was her own very evident zest for life, her high spirits, her sense of fun, her cheerful acceptance of all she couldn't do, her delight in what little she could. She set us an example and taught us a philosophy that parents don't usually expect to learn from their children.'

'We tend to think that, if someone is deprived of a blessing that we ourselves possess, their life is the sadder. This is particularly so in today's Age of Equality, where we are made to feel almost guilty at having what others do not have. But in fact, the man who has less than his neighbour is only unhappy if he had been hoping for more and chooses to feel jealous.'

'Is it sad that there is so little that Clare can do? Not necessarily. There are plenty of things that even the most agile person cannot do. Happiness is not measured by agility.'[2]

'When the question arose: who is going to look after Clare now that she is growing up and cannot look after herself? the answer was obvious:

"We are". And if this meant there were other things that in consequence we couldn't do, then we didn't do them.'[3]

Christopher considered himself well-equipped to look after Clare:

'Anyone who was taking door locks to bits at the age of seven to find out how they worked, who at the age of eleven was inventing burglar alarms for a secret passage, and who was happily defusing German mines at the age of twenty-three, was obviously the right sort of father to have when Clare, sleeping alone in her bedroom, waking in the morning and unable to get out of bed, needed a word with her parents. An electric bell that she could work and then - to make a voice pipe – a plastic funnel and a length of garden hose … The amateur inventor, gadget maker, and general handyman was in his element.'[4]

And Christopher demonstrated his caring nature by providing Clare with some furniture to suit her requirements:

'Why should Clare not have as many chairs as we have? Why should she not take the pride and pleasure in them that we take in ours? Why should they not be every bit as decorative and pleasing to look at? No reason at all. They couldn't be bought, of course; but they could be made. And so I set to work to make them.'

'When I first started carpentry lessons at school, the pleasure I got was the pleasure of cutting and shaping the wood. The lines were ruled for me, and I sawed along them and chiselled between them. At John Lewis [department store] I began to look at furniture rather more critically. Some I liked; some I disliked. But it was not until I was puzzling over Clare's needs that I discovered another pleasure as great as the pleasure of making: the pleasure of designing.'[5]

'But of course, the greatest pleasure of all was to see Clare sitting comfortably where before she had been uncomfortable, doing something she had not previously been able to do. And it was a pleasant thought that this was, in a sense, a legacy from her grandparents whom she had never known – a product of the fusion of my father's fondness for mathematics with my mother's competent hands. If she [Clare] had inherited neither, she could at least benefit from the fact that I had inherited both.'[6] At least there was *something* for which Christopher was grateful to his parents for!

From the age of 5 to the age of 17 (1961-1973), Clare attended school.

'All children limit the freedom of their parents to some extent. And in fact, Clare limited ours less than most. For at the age of five she went to school, and since this had to be a special school, it had also to be a boarding school. Very luckily there was one conveniently close, the Dame Hannah Rogers School at Ivybridge, twenty miles away on the edge of Dartmoor.'

The school was founded in 1767 through the generous legacy of Dame Hannah, wife of Sir John Rogers, MP for Plymouth.

'So our lives fell into that pattern that Lesley and I both knew so well from our own school days, the alternation between term time and holidays; with all the misery that attends the approach of the one, and all the bliss that heralds the other. For Clare, the depths and the heights were probably no less and no more than they had been for us.'[7]

When his mother Daphne died in 1971, said 'Christopher, 'From now on a part of my father's royalties would be coming to me. So, the spur had gone'.[8] In other words, for Christopher, there was no longer any necessity for him to earn his own living. But he continued to do so, nonetheless.

Christopher and Lesley's 'Harbour Bookshop' in Dartmouth 'opened its doors' on 25 August 1951.[9] In 1972, Christopher stated that:

'For twenty-one years Lesley and I lived on the profits of our shop, and the bulk of this came from bookselling. We had no other source of income. I say this loudly and proudly. Loudly, because a number of people seem to have suspected that all the while Pooh's earnings were keeping my pockets comfortably lined. Proudly, because it is not easy to survive as a bookseller - in fact as well as in name - in a town whose population is under seven thousand.'[10] The bookshop 'had been our sole source of income. We had proved to ourselves that we could do it: that we could survive as booksellers here in Dartmouth'.[11]

During Clare's time at school, said Christopher in 1973:

'They had taught her a lot of things … though not as much as some children learn. But they had not taught her how to walk. School was now finished. Clare would be living at home, and I would be helping to look after her. So, I could no longer be a full-time bookseller.'[12] Furthermore:

'However, much I might wish to be independent, standing on my own feet, I was very much aware that this, both figuratively and literally, was something Clare would never be able to do. So here was a dilemma. Fortunately, it was not one that called for an immediate decision. It would be a long while before probate [on his late father's estate] had been settled, leaving my emotions plenty of time to sort themselves out inside me.'[13]

When Clare had been at boarding school, said Christopher:

'Lesley and I had both of us been full-time booksellers for three-quarters of the year. For the other quarter, the school holidays, I had worked in the mornings, she in the afternoons. What was going to happen now! 'For the time being, at any rate, Clare would be living at home: this was what we all three wanted. She had spent little enough of her life at home, and we had spent little enough of ours with her; and now we would make up for it. In any case, there wasn't any very acceptable alternative. This meant that Lesley would have to remain a permanent part-time bookseller. As for me, I still had half a book to finish.'[14]

This was Christopher's autobiography *The Enchanted Places*, published in 1974. Writing it, he said, was like enduring 'a session on the analyst's couch'. However:

'In my case the writing and its reception combined to lift me from under the shadow of my father and of Christopher Robin, and to my surprise and pleasure I found myself standing beside them in the sunshine, able to look them both in the eye.'[15] Christopher had evidently, at long last, overcome his crippling inferiority complex in respect of his father Alan.

Even though he was now a professional writer, said Christopher:

'I doubt if it leads me on to fortune and luckily it doesn't need to; for I have accepted my namesake's offer of help. I had to accept it for Clare's sake, of course. But perhaps I might need to accept it for my sake and for Lesley's as well. For although one might measure the ability of a bookseller by what he earns, this has never been the measure of a writer.'[16]

In other words, Christopher had decided to accept his share of the royalties from the sale of his father's books featuring 'Christopher Robin'.
However, he subsequently sold his rights to future royalties to the Royal Literary Fund and used the capital to set up a trust fund for Clare.

Could Christopher and Lesley have foreseen that having a child might have such disastrous consequences, given the fact that being first cousins, they were so closely related? They were both educated and knowledgeable people so probably, yes.

In an article entitled 'The Genetics of Cousin Marriage', US biologist James MacDonald stated as follows:

'We each receive one copy of each gene from each of our parents. Thus, we inherit two versions of each gene (called alleles); one can be dominant and the other recessive. For a recessive gene to actually manifest in an individual, both copies of the gene must be the recessive allele. If an individual inherits only one recessive allele of the gene, the individual is considered a carrier who can pass on the potential for illness to their offspring. But when an individual inherits two copies of a dangerous recessive allele, the gene is said to be unmasked and he or she will inherit the condition.'[17] Either way it is a 'no win' situation.

In 2005, Owen Dyer, journalist at British Medical Journal, reported that British researchers had:

'formally crunched the numbers and determined that for any given individual, with much variation, a marriage between first cousins roughly doubles the rate of unmasking compared to nonrelative marriages (~6% instead of ~3%).'[18]

In 2018, V. Souma of GITAM University, West Bengal and her colleagues stated that 'Consanguinity, birth asphyxia', and 'neonatal jaundice are found to be the important risk factors for Cerebral Palsy.'[19]

'Consanguineous' is defined as relating to or denoting people descended from the same ancestor.[20] So, was consanguinity the reason for Clare's cerebral palsy? Evidently so, there being no mention of either neonatal jaundice or birth complications in the accounts given.

Although the marriage of first cousins is legal in the United Kingdom, such marriages are illegal in about half of the states of the USA for the reasons mentioned above.

Finally, Christopher revealed his deep and abiding love for Clare in the last few lines of his book, *The Path Through The Trees*, published in 1979, where he and she are going to meet her mother on her return from the bookshop. "Which is it to be: tricycle or wheelchair?' he says:

'I grip Clare round her waist and she puts her arms around my neck and I hoist her up. Comfortable? And away we go, slowly because the path is a little slippery, down through the trees.'[21]

In 1998, Clare received a significant sum of money following the sale of the copyright royalties from her grandfather's books. Whereupon a home was purchased for her in Otterton, East Devon.

Chapter 34

The Clare Milne Trust

When Christopher Milne was young, said Gyles Brandreth, who knew both him and his wife Lesley, money:

'didn't interest him. When he was older, he was grateful for his share of the millions that came with the Disney [US entertainment and media conglomerate] acquisition of the rights to Pooh & Co.' In 1961, Walt Disney Productions obtained the license for certain films and other rights to the Winnie-the-Pooh characters, stories and trademarks, from US radio, television and film producer Stephen Slesinger, Inc. and the estate of A. A. Milne.

'This enabled Christopher and Lesley to establish a charity for people with disabilities that does good work in the West Country to this day.'[1]

'The Clare Milne Trust (established in 2002) supports people living with disabilities in Devon and Cornwall. The Trust does this by making grants to charities working directly with people with disabilities in the South West. The Clare Milne Trust focuses its grants on small effective charities with good volunteer support.'

Clare sadly died on 27 October 2012, 'but her legacy continues.'

In the words of Clare's late mother, Lesley Milne, 'My dream is to know that my girl will be remembered for something that brings happiness where it is most needed'.

'The current Trustees strive to honour Lesley's wishes and to keep Clare's memory alive.'[2]

Chapter 35

Christopher Milne: A Reluctant Celebrity

When his mother Daphne died on 24 March 1971, aged 81, said Christopher:

'My reaction was not typically that of a child who has lost a parent. There was little sadness, little sense of bereavement. How could there be? I had last seen her at my father's memorial service, and we had scarcely written to each other since.'

'On my father's death my mother had taken over responsibility for his estate. If any decisions were to be made, they were hers to make. I was two hundred miles away and only too relieved to be able to say to enquirers, "I am afraid it is nothing to do with me".'

'When Cotchford was sold, I knew only when her next letter came from a London address. No, my chief concern was that a part of my father's royalties would now be mine – and I didn't want it.' In this age of materialism, Christopher's attitude was far from typical!

'It is easy to give. It is extremely hard to receive. I am bad at receiving, bad at having to be grateful. I like to be able to boast to myself that what I have done I have done without help. Hence my insistence that I was a professional bookseller, and that the bookshop was the sole source of our income. Hence my anger when anyone implied that they thought I was only a dilettante, not really having to make the business pay, happily able to rely on a private income.'

'But in spite of my determination to earn my own living, I looked upon what I earned more as a measure of my ability to sell books than anything else. I didn't particularly welcome the money for its own sake or for the sake of what it would buy. My ambition was to be a good rather than a rich bookseller: there was something not quite nice about being rich.'

'Whether or not this attitude is understandable, it does, I hope, explain why a sudden, relatively large, and unearned addition to our income was not at all what I wanted. Many dream of winning the football pools. For me this would be nightmare. To travel hopefully being a better thing than to arrive, I didn't welcome the offer of a lift. No, thank you, I prefer to walk. How often have I said this!'

'To be offered a lift by anybody would therefore have been bad enough, and I would have been tempted to decline it. But to be offered a lift by, of all people, my fictional namesake, to have to travel the rest of my way in *his* company – this was the final insult to my injured pride.'[1]

But had not Christopher once said that his father 'had got to where he was by climbing upon my infant shoulders'? So, if Christopher had contributed to Milne's success, which he clearly believed to be the case, then why was he loath to share in the proceeds of that success?

Christopher's petulant and resentful attitude, towards his father Alan and to his father's success and new-found wealth, is difficult to explain. After all, when Milne wrote the Pooh books he had no idea just how successful they would be. In fact, he also resented their success, on the grounds that this overshadowed what continued to be his main vocation, that of playwright and poet. Furthermore, Christopher either ignored or failed to understand that Milne's poems and stories featuring 'Christopher Robin' reflected the author's deep and abiding love for his son. And this at a time when, because of the presence of Nanny Brockwell, or because of his self-confessed shyness, Milne was not able to demonstrate this love as openly as he surely would have wished.

Furthermore, as already mentioned, when Milne was asked what effect being a 'household name' had had on his son, he had replied, as already mentioned, that 'it had done him no harm, might even have done some good', and that Christopher 'seemed perfectly happy.'

For who, on reading Milne's 'Vespers', could fail to notice that the love of a father for his son, permeated every line of that poem.

What if Christopher had adopted an entirely different attitude, regarded it as an honour and privilege to have been immortalized in a book by a loving father who only ever wished the best for him? Surely then, this would have made for a far more harmonious relationship between the two generations.

Epilogue

A. A. Milne

A. A. Milne died in 1956, at the age of seventy- four, 'having been an invalid since suffering a stroke several years earlier', said Campbell. Although he and Shepard 'were never personal friends', they 'had kept in touch over the years, not least due to joint business issues connected to the Pooh stories, and Shepard was saddened by the end of a long-standing professional collaboration that had achieved so much for so many.'[1]

E. H. Shepard

After the end of the Second World War, said Campbell:

'Shepard was as busy as ever. He continued as principal cartoonist for *Punch* for a further ten years, documenting the political upheavals of the 1940s Labour government, many of which would define the post-war era in Britain - including the creation of the National Health Service and the widespread nationalisation of key public services. He continued to draw illustrations for books and he designed dust jackets and worked on a range of projects and activities that would have exhausted a man half his age.'[2]

However, in 1954, when journalist and satirist Malcolm Muggeridge replaced Kenneth Bird as editor, Shepard was dismissed 'after nearly fifty years of regular contributions to *Punch* and nearly twenty as chief cartoonist'.[3] In 1955 Shepard and his wife Norah relocated to Lodsworth near Midhurst in Sussex.[4]

In *Drawn from Memory* (1957), Shepard described a single year during his childhood and in *Drawn From Life* (1961), he described the period from his schooldays to his marriage to Florence in 1904.

In the mid-1960s, Shepard turned his hand to writing and illustrating children's books, for example *Ben and Brock* (1965) and *Betsy and Joe* (1966), 'both delightful pastoral tales'.[5]

In 1972 Shepard was awarded the OBE (Officer of the Order of the British Empire) in the Queen's Birthday Honours, the citation being 'Artist and Illustrator'.

Shepard died on 24 March 1976 at the age of 96. His widow Norah died in 1977.

Christopher Milne

'Christopher Robin Milne maintained a friendly relationship with Shepard', said Campbell:

'exchanging occasional letters and Christmas cards, and in 1974 sent him a copy of his reminiscences, *The Enchanted Places*, with the inscription, 'For Ernest Shepard, who added so much of his own very special magic to that of the Enchanted Places'.

Christopher also sent a charming letter to Shepard with a private 'thank you' to him for everything he had done:

'Dear Mr Shepard,

This is to remind you of how and where it all started and – I hope – to revive some happy memories of Cotchford Farm and of my parents.'[6]

In his later years, Christopher Milne suffered from myasthenia gravis, a condition causing abnormal weakness of the muscles of the face, throat, and elsewhere. Christopher died on 20 April 1996. His widow Lesley died in September of that year.

Gyles Brandreth said:

'At the beginning and, more importantly, at the end of his life, Christopher was quite happy with who he was. I know because he told me.'

'When I first got to know him in the 1980s, Christopher had just turned sixty. He seemed older. He was a little bent, with owlish glasses and a mischievous twinkle in his eye. I had been warned that I would find him painfully shy, diffident about his parents, reluctant to talk about Pooh. In fact, he was consciously charming, gentle but forthcoming. He said at once, "Of course, we must talk about Pooh. It's been something of a love-hate relationship down the years, but it's all right now. Believe it or not, I can look at those four books without flinching. I'm quite fond of them really".'

'Christopher told me that, until he was eight or nine, he "quite liked being famous".' Subsequently, however, said Brandreth, he believed (as already mentioned) that his father:

'had got where he was by climbing on my infant shoulders, that he had filched from me my good name and had left me with nothing but the empty fame of being his son.'

That's how he felt then, but it's not how he felt later. 'I don't want to blame my parents for anything', he told me.

'In his father's final years', said Brandreth, 'Christopher rarely saw him. "My father's heart remained buttoned-up", he said, "but I know he loved me and, of course, I loved him. And, yes, I loved Pooh, too".'

Brandreth continued:

'And in that enchanted place on the top of the forest', I asked him, 'a little boy and his bear will always be playing?'

'I expect so', he smiled. 'I don't mind.'[7]

And so it is for millions throughout the world, who imagine a little boy and his bear, forever young, forever companions, forever friends.

Notes

Introduction

1. Milne, A. A., *When We Were Very Young* and *Now We Are Six*, illustrated by E. H. Shepard, p.156.
2. *Ibid,* p.243.

Chapter 1: Roger Lancelyn Green and the 'Golden Age' of Children's Books

1. Essays, p.59.
2. Grahame, Kenneth, *The Golden Age*.
3. Soanes, Catherine and Angus Stevenson (Editors), *Oxford Dictionary of English*. ODE.
4. Grahame, Kenneth, *The Golden Age*, op. cit.
5. Essays, p.64.
6. Angela Sorby, in Adrian Munsey's *Wonderland*, Odyssey Television, 2022. Sky Arts.

Chapter 2: *Alice's Adventures in Wonderland* and the Dawn of the 'Golden Age' of Children's Books

1. Soanes, Catherine and Angus Stevenson (Editors), *Oxford Dictionary of English*.
2. Milne, A. A., *Year in, Year Out*, p.13.
3. Ibid, p.16.

Chapter 3: Some Male Authors from the 'Golden Age' of Children's Books

1. Flood, Alison, 'Kipling's Poignant Jungle Book Inscription Comes to Light', 9 April 2010, *The Guardian* online.
2. Millgate, Michael (editor), *Letters of Emma and Florence Hardy*, Emma Hardy to Elspeth Grahame, 20 August 1899.
3. Graham, Kenneth, *My Dearest Mouse: The Wind in the Willows Letters*, p.9.
4. Ibid, p.11.
5. Ibid, p.19.
6. Ibid, p.56.
7. Ibid, p.64.
8. Prince, Alison, *Kenneth Grahame: An Innocent in the Wild Wood*, p.238.
9. Milne, A. A., *Not That It Matters*, pp.87-89.
10. Shepard's War pp.137-8,140.
11. Graham, Kenneth, *My Dearest Mouse: The Wind in the Willows Letters*, op. cit., p.36.
12. Shepard's War pp.137-8,140.
13. Barrie, J. M., *Margaret Ogilvy by Her Son* (Hodder & Stoughton, London, 1897).

Chapter 4: Some Female Authors from the 'Golden Age' of Children's Books

1. Winter, Jessica, 'The British Socialist who Rewrote the World for Children', *The New Yorker*, 28 September 2022.
2. Soanes, Catherine and Angus Stevenson (Editors), *Oxford Dictionary of English.*
3. Merriam-Webster dictionary online.
4. James, William (1929), *The Varieties of Religious Experience*, pp. 92–3.
5. Burnett, Frances Hodgson, interview for *The New York Times*, 12 October 1913.
6. McCarthy, Michael Francis: 'Forget the Devil and Keep Your Pink Lamps Lighted: The Metaphysics of Frances Hodgson Burnett's The Secret Garden', 'The Looking Glass: New Perspectives on Children's Literature': 1, Volume 14, No 1, 2010.

Chapter 5: The Aforementioned 'Golden Age' Authors Compared

1. Soanes, Catherine and Angus Stevenson (Editors), *Oxford Dictionary of English.*

Chapter 7: Cricket

1. Telfer, Kevin, *Peter Pan's First XI*, p.247.
2. Stevenson, A., and Waite, M., *Concise Oxford English Dictionary* (Oxford University Press, 2011)
3. Telfer, Kevin, op. cit., p.13.
4. Ibid, p.19.
5. Barrie, J. M., *The Greenwood Hat* , p.96.
6. Barrie, J. M., *Allahakbarries C. C. 1899*, pp.39-40.
7. Telfer, Kevin, op. cit., p.172.
8. Barrie, J. M., *Allahakbarries C. C. 1899*, p.37.
9. Stevenson, A., and Waite, M., op. cit.
10. Telfer, Kevin, op. cit., p.172.
11. Milne, A. A., *It's Too Late Now*, p.153.

Chapter 8: A. A. Milne and *Punch* Magazine

1. Milne, A. A., *It's Too Late Now*, p.167.
2. Ibid, p.167.
3. Ibid, p.168.
4. Ibid, p.169.
5. Ibid, p.198.
6. Ibid, p.205.

Chapter 9: The First World War (1914-1918): Milne Enlists

1. Milne, A. A., *It's Too Late Now*, p.212.
2. Milne, A. A., *Year in, Year Out*, p.206.
3. Kendall-Carpenter, Nick, *Roger So Far: The First 100 years of the Royal Corps of Signals*, p.22.

4. Milne, A. A., *It's Too Late Now*, op. cit., p.212.
5. Ibid, p.213.

Chapter 10: Types of Signalling Equipment

1. Kendall-Carpenter, Nick, *Roger So Far: The First 100 years of the Royal Corps of Signals*, p.26.
2. Stevenson, A., and Waite, M., *Concise Oxford English Dictionary.*
3. Kendall-Carpenter, Nick, op. cit., p.22.
4. 'A Signaller in World War 1', worcestershireregiment.com, online.
5. Kendall-Carpenter, Nick, op. cit., p.26.
6. Stevenson, A., and Waite, M., op. cit.
7. 'A Signaller in World War 1', worcestershireregiment.com, online.
8. Kendall-Carpenter, Nick, op. cit., p.24.
9. Ibid, p.24.
10. Ibid, p.25.

Chapter 11: The Task of the Signaller

1. Kendall-Carpenter, Nick, *Roger So Far: The First 100 years of the Royal Corps of Signals*, p.19.
2. Ibid, p.26.

Chapter 12: Milne Goes Into Action

1. Kendall-Carpenter, Nick, *Roger So Far: The First 100 years of the Royal Corps of Signals*.
2. Milne, A. A., *It's Too Late Now*, p.215.
3. Ibid, p.217.
4. Ibid, p.217.
5. Ibid, pp.217-8.
6. Priestley, R. E., Work of R. E. in The European War, 1914-1918: The Signal Service (France) (Naval & Military Press, Uckfield, East Sussex, UK, 2006)
7. Milne, A. A., op. cit., pp.217-8.
8. Ibid, pp.218-9.

9. Ibid, pp.219-220.
10. Ibid, pp.222-3.
11. Ibid, p.223.
12. Ibid, p.223-4.
13. Ibid, p.224.
14. Ibid, p.225.
15. 'A. A. Milne: A Signals Officer During WW1: From the Somme to Hundred Acre Wood', **info@royalsignalsmuseum.co.uk**

Chapter 13: MI7b: *The Green Book*

1. Milne, A. A., *It's Too Late Now*, pp.225-6.
2. MI7b & *The Green Book.*
3. 'The Corpse Factory and the Birth of Fake News' BBC News, 17 February 2017.
4. MI7b & *The Green Book*
5. Royal Signals Museum Information Pamphlet Number 29, 'The Green Book: MI7b – Captain James Lloyd'
6. Extract from *The Green Book*, by kind permission of Jeremy Arter.

Chapter 14: The War Ends

1. Milne, A. A., *It's Too Late Now*, pp.229-30.
2. Campbell, James, *The Art of Winnie-The-Pooh*, p.32.
3. Milne, A. A., op. cit., pp.232-3.
4. Ibid, p.233.
5. Ibid, p.333.
6. Ibid, p.234.
7. Ibid, p.235.
8. Milne, Christopher, *The Enchanted Places*, pp.13-14.
9. Milne, A. A., op. cit, pp.236-7.
10. Ibid, pp.235-6.
11. Ibid, p.237.
12. Ibid, p.237.
13. Campbell, James, op. cit., p.34.

Chapter 15: Milne and the First World War: Shell Shock

1. Milne, A. A., *It's Too Late Now*, p.211.
2. Stevenson, A., and Waite, M., *Concise Oxford English Dictionary.*
3. 'Shell Shock', *Wikipedia.*
4. Jones, Edgar, Dr, 'Shell-Shocked', American Psychological Association, June 2012, Volume 43, Number 6.
5. Stevenson, A., and Waite, M., op. cit.
6. Myers, Charles S., 'A Contribution to the Study of Shell Shock: Being an Account of Three Cases of Loss of Memory, Vision, Smell, and Taste, Admitted into the Duchess of Westminster's War Hospital, Le Touquet', *The Lancet*, Volume 185, Number 13, February 1915, pp.316-320.
7. Jones, Edgar, Dr, op. cit.
8. 'Shell Shock', BBC, 'Inside Out Extra', 3 March 2004.
9. A. A. Milne Poetry of the Great War, 16 December 2019, online.
10. Myers, Major Charles S., 'Contributions to the Study of Shell Shock', *The Lancet*, 8 January 1916.
11. 'Cognitive Behavioural Therapy', *Wikipedia.*

Chapter 16: Christopher Robin Milne (born 21 August 1920)

1. Milne, Christopher, *The Enchanted Places*, p.36.
2. Ibid, p.49.
3. Ibid, p.17.
4. Ibid, p.49.
5. Ibid, p.51.
6. Ibid, p.33.
7. Ibid, p.88.
8. Ibid, p.80.

Chapter 17: More About Christopher and His Father Alan

1. Milne, Christopher, *The Enchanted Places*, p.17.
2. Ibid, p.42.

3. Ibid, pp.108-9.
4. Ibid, p.121.
5. Ibid, p.121.
6. Ibid, p.125.
7. Ibid, p.125.
8. Ibid, p.125
9. Ibid, p.141.
10. Ibid, p.141.
11. Ibid, p.39.
12. Ibid, p.39.
13. Ibid, p.39.
14. Ibid, pp.121-2.
15. Ibid, p.40.
16. Ibid, p.41.
17. Ibid, p.41.
18. Ibid, pp.30-31.

Chapter 18: Christopher and His Mother Dorothy ('Daphne')

1. Milne, Christopher, *The Enchanted Places*, pp.16-17.
2. Ibid, p.37.
3. Ibid, p.38.
4. Ibid, p.38.
5. Ibid, p.38.

Chapter 19: What Motivated Milne to Write?

1. Milne, Christopher, *The Enchanted Places*, pp.9-10.
2. Ibid, pp.9-10.
3. Stevenson, A., and Waite, M., *Concise Oxford English Dictionary*.
4. Milne, Christopher, op. cit., p.10.

Chapter 20: Milne and Shepard Meet (Autumn 1923): E. V. Lucas - The Catalyst

1. Shepard, E. H., *Drawn From Life*, p.122.
2. Milne, A. A., *By Way of Introduction*, pp.25–6.

3. Lucas, E. V., *Reading, Writing and Remembering*, p.319.
4. Ibid, pp.318-9.

Chapter 21: More About E. H. Shepard

1. Shepard, E. H., *Drawn From Life*, p.13.
2. Ibid, p.7.
3. Campbell, James, *Shepard's War*, p.20.
4. Shepard, E. H., op. cit., p.15.
5. Ibid, p.8.
6. Ibid, p.17.
7. Ibid, p.23.
8. Ibid, p.26.
9. Ibid, p.7.
10. Ibid, p.36.
11. Ibid, p.12.
12. Ibid, p.53.
13. Campbell, James, *Shepard's War*, p.21.
14. Shepard, E. H., op. cit., p.79.
15. Ibid, p.17
16. Ibid, pp.78-9.
17. Campbell, James, *Shepard's War*, p.21.
18. Shepard, E. H., op. cit., p.121.
19. 'Royal Academy of Arts', *Wikipedia*.
20. Shepard, E. H., op. cit., p.122.
21. Ibid, p.128.
22. Ibid, p.151
23. Ibid, p.162.
24. Ibid, p.179.
25. Campbell, James, *Shepard's War*, pp.22-3.
26. Shepard, E. H., op. cit., p.183.
27. Ibid, p.179.
28. Ibid, p.188.
29. Ibid, pp. 198-9.
30. Campbell, James, *The Art of Winnie-The-Pooh*, p.22.
31. 'E. H Shepard', *Wikipedia*.

Chapter 22: E. H. Shepard and the First World War (1914-1918)

1. Campbell, James, *The Art of Winnie-The-Pooh*, p.22.
2. 'E. H. Shepard', *Wikipedia.*
3. Campbell, James, *Shepard's War*, p.91.
4. Ibid, p.69.

Chapter 23: Shepard's brother Cyril and the Folly of War.

1. 'Devonshire Cemetery', Commonwealth War Graves Commission.
2. 'Captain Duncan Lenox Martin, 9th Battalion, The Devonshire Regiment', The Keep Military Museum, Dorchester, Dorset online.
3. 'Epitaphs of the Great War' online.
4. Turner, Camilla, The London Telegraph, The Listening Post, Issue 67, Summer 2016.

Chapter 24: E. V. Lucas and the First World War

1. Lucas, E. V., *Reading, Writing and Remembering*, p.278.
2. Ibid, p.283.
3. Ibid, p.288.

Chapter 25: E. H. Shepard and the Lost Wartime Sketches

1. Turner, Camilla, 'First World War Sketches by Winnie-the-Pooh Illustrator Discovered in Trunk', The London Telegraph, The Listening Post, Issue 67, Summer 2016.
2. Campbell, James, *Shepard's War*, pp.62,80.
3. Stevenson, A., and Waite, M., *Concise Oxford English Dictionary.*
4. Campbell, James, op. cit., p.75.
5. Corcoran. Kieran, 'Poignant sketches by Winnie-the-Pooh illustrator E. H. Shepard of the First World War trenches are discovered in a trunk that had not been opened for almost 100 years', MailOnline, 30 January 2015.

Chapter 26: 'Pooh' and 'Christopher Robin' Make Their Debut

1. Campbell, James, *The Art of Winnie-The-Pooh*, p.52.
2. Ibid, p.59.
3. Colebourn, Fred, 'Biographical Sketch' of his father Harry Colebourn, in 'Remembering the Real Winnie: the World's Most Famous Bear Turns 100', Ryerson University, Toronto, Canada.
4. 'Winnie-the-Pooh: A Bear of Little Brain', Royal Signals Information Pamphlet Number 28.

Chapter 27: Enter E. H. Shepard, and 'Pooh' and 'Christopher Robin' Come to Life!

1. Campbell, James, *The Art of Winnie-The-Pooh*, p.40.
2. Ibid, pp.46,49.
3. Ibid, p.53.
4. Milne, Christopher, *The Enchanted Places*, p.84.
5. *When We Were Very Young* and Now Six, P.13.
6. Milne, Christopher, op. cit., p.68.

Chapter 28: The Characters and Their Locations

1. Milne, Christopher, *The Enchanted Places*, p.54.
2. Ibid, p.55.
3. Ibid, p.55.
4. Ibid, p.55.
5. Ibid, p.56.
6. Ibid, p.65.
7. Ibid, p.67.
8. Ibid, p.68.
9. Campbell, James, *The Art of Winnie-The-Pooh*, p.61.
10. Ibid, p.107.
11. Ibid, p.61

Chapter 29: Success, But at What Cost?

1. Milne, Christopher, *The Enchanted Places*, pp.144-5.
2. Ibid, p.146.
3. Thwaite, Ann, *A. A. Milne: His Life*, p.469.
4. Ibid, p.471.
5. Melrose, A. R. (editor), *Beyond the World of Pooh*, p.178.
6. Milne, Christopher, op. cit., p.148.
7. Ibid, p.148.
8. Melrose, A. R., op. cit., p.187.
9. Ibid, p.259.
10. Brandreth, Gyles, 'Now we are 100: the truth about Christopher Robin', 19 August 2020, online.
11. Art p.139.

Chapter 30: From Milne's Perspective

1. Milne, A. A., *By Way of Introduction*, p.204.
2. Ibid, pp.204-5.

Chapter 31: Aftermath

1. Campbell, James, *The Art of Winnie-The-Pooh*, p.116.
2. Campbell, James, *Shepard's War*, p.132.
3. Ibid, pp.133, 136.
4. Ibid, p.136.
5. Ibid, p.136.
6. Campbell, James, *The Art of Winnie-The-Pooh*, p.120.
7. Campbell, James, *The Art of Winnie-The-Pooh*, p.119.

Chapter 32: The Second World War (1939-1945)

1. Campbell, James, *The Art of Winnie-The-Pooh*, p.121.
2. Campbell, James, *Shepard's War*, p.121.
3. Ibid, p.142.

4. Ibid, p.142.
5. Ibid, p.143.
6. Ibid, p.130.
7. Melrose, A. R. (editor), *Beyond the World of Pooh*, p.119.
8. Ibid, p.128.
9. Ibid, p.132.
10. Ibid, p.137.
11. Ibid, pp.144-5.
12. Ibid, p.147.
13. Stevenson, A., and Waite, M., *Concise Oxford English Dictionary*.
14. Melrose, A. R. (editor), *Beyond the World of Pooh*, pp.151-2.
15. Ibid, p.154.
16. Ibid, p.155.

Chapter 33: Clare Milne (born June 1956)

1. Stevenson, A., and Waite, M., *Concise Oxford English Dictionary*.
2. Melrose, A. R. (editor), *Beyond the World of Pooh*, pp.238-9.
3. Ibid, p.240.
4. Ibid, p.242.
5. Ibid, p.244.
6. Ibid, p.245
7. Ibid, p.240.
8. Ibid, p.237.
9. Ibid, p.199.
10. Ibid, p.218.
11. Ibid, p.237.
12. Ibid, p.237.
13. Ibid, p.260.
14. Ibid, p.264
15. Ibid, pp.267-8.
16. Ibid, p.268.
17. MacDonald, James, 'The Genetics of Cousin Marriage', JSTOR Daily, online, 20 August 2018.
18. Dyer, Owen, 'MP Is Criticised for saying that Marriage of First Cousins is a Health Problem', British Medical Journal, Volume 331, Number 7528, p.1292, 3 December 2005.

19. Soumya, V., et al., 'A study on maternal and perinatal risk factors of cerebral palsy among children attending a cerebral palsy clinic in Visakhapatnam', International Journal of Community Medicine and Public Health, (1), pp.317-325, January 2018
20. Stevenson, A., and Waite, M., op. cit.
21. Milne, Christopher, *The Path Through The Trees*, p.287.

Chapter 34: The Clare Milne Trust

1. Brandreth, Gyles, 'Now we are 100: The Truth About Christopher Robin', 19 August 2020, online.
2. 'Clare Milne and The Clare Milne Trust', online.

Chapter 35: Christopher Milne: A Reluctant Celebrity

1. Melrose, A. R. (editor), *Beyond the World of Pooh*, pp.259-60.

Epilogue

1. Campbell, James, *The Art of Winnie-The-Pooh*, p.126.
2. Ibid, p.123.
3. Campbell, James, *Shepard's War*, p.146.
4. Ibid, p.147.
5. Ibid, pp.148-9.
6. Campbell, James, *The Art of Winnie-The-Pooh*, Op. cit., pp.137-8.
7. Brandreth, Gyles, 'Now we are 100: the truth about Christopher Robin', 19 August 2020, online.

Bibliography

A Dorset Childhood: Growing up in the Land of the Tolpuddle Martyrs at the Time of the Cold War, Pen & Sword, 2023.

A Purbeck Romance: Set in Thomas Hardy's Glorious Wessex, Pen & Sword, 2023.

Allen, David Rayvern, *Peter Pan and Cricket* (Constable, London, 1988).

Authors XI (Bloomsbury, London, 2013).

Barrie, J. M., *Allahakbarries C. C. 1899* (James Barrie, London, 1950).

Barrie, J. M., *The Greenwood Hat* (Peter Davies, London, 1937).

Campbell, James, *The Art of Winnie-The-Pooh* (LOM Art, London, 2017).

Campbell, James, *Shepard's War* (LOM Art, London, 2015).

Grahame, Kenneth, *The Golden Age* (The Bodley Head, London, 1875).

Grahame, Kenneth, *My Dearest Mouse: The Wind in the Willows Letters* (Pavilion Books, London, 1988).

Green, Roger Lancelyn, *The Golden Age of Children's Books* (John Murray, London, 1962).

Green, Roger Lancelyn, *Tellers of Tales* (Kaye & Ward, London, 1969).

James, William, *The Varieties of Religious Experience* (Modern Library, New York City, 1929).

Kendall-Carpenter, Nick, *Roger So Far: The First 100 years of the Royal Corps of Signals* (History Press, Cheltenham, UK, 2020).

Lucas, E. V., *Cricket All His Life: The Cricket Writings of E. V. Lucas* (Rupert Hart-Davis, London, 1950).

Lucas, E. V., *Reading, Writing and Remembering* (Methuen, London, 1932).

Melrose, A. R. (Editor), *Beyond the World of Pooh* (Methuen, London, 1988).

Milne, A. A., *By Way of Introduction* (Methuen, London, 1929).

Milne, A. A., *It's Too Late Now* (Methuen, London, 1939).

Milne, A. A., *Not That It Matters* (Methuen, London, 1921).

Milne, A. A., *The Complete Winnie-the-Pooh*, containing *Winnie-the-Pooh* and *The House at Pooh Corner*, illustrated by E. H. Shepard (Dean, London, 2002).

Milne, A. A., *When We Were Very Young* and *Now We Are Six*, illustrated by E. H. Shepard (Dean, London, 2002).

Milne, A. A., *Year in, Year Out* (Methuen, London, 1952).

Milne, Christopher, *The Enchanted Places* (Pan Books, London, 1974).

Milne, Christopher, *The Path Through The Trees* (Eyre Methuen, London, 1979).

Prince, Alison, *Kenneth Grahame: An Innocent in the Wild Wood* (Faber & Faber, London, 1994).

Shepard, E. H., *Drawn From Life* (Methuen, London, 2002).

Shepard, E. H., *Drawn From Memory* (Methuen, London, 2000).

Soanes, Catherine and Angus Stevenson (Editors), *Oxford Dictionary of English* (Oxford University Press, 2006).

Stevenson, A., and Waite, M. (Editors), *Concise Oxford English Dictionary* (Oxford University Press, 2011)

Telfer, Kevin, *Peter Pan's First XI* (Sceptre, London, 2010)

Thwaite, Ann, *A. A. Milne: His Life* (Faber and Faber, London, 1991).

The Real Sir Arthur Conan Doyle, Pen & Sword, 2023.

Thomas Hardy and the Death of Emma: What His Writings Reveal, Pen & Sword, 2024.

White, Beatrice, (collector of) *Essays and Studies* (John Murray, London, 1962).

By the same author

By Swords Divided: Corfe Castle in the Civil War. Halsgrove, 2003.

Thomas Hardy: Christmas Carollings. Halsgrove, 2005.

Enid Blyton and her Enchantment with Dorset. Halsgrove, 2005.

Tyneham: A Tribute. Halsgrove, 2007.

Agatha Christie: The Finished Portrait. Tempus, 2007.

The Story of George Loveless and the Tolpuddle Martyrs. Halsgrove, 2008.

Father of the Blind: A Portrait of Sir Arthur Pearson. The History Press, 2009.

Agatha Christie: The Pitkin Guide. Pitkin Publishing, 2009.

Arthur Conan Doyle: The Man behind Sherlock Holmes. The History Press, 2009.

HMS Hood: Pride of the Royal Navy. The History Press, 2009.

Purbeck Personalities. Halsgrove, 2009. *Bournemouth's Founders and Famous Visitors*. The History Press, 2010.

Thomas Hardy: Behind the Mask. The History Press, 2011.

A Brummie Boy goes to War. Halsgrove, 2011. *Winston Churchill: Portrait of an Unquiet Mind*. Pen & Sword Books, 2012.

Charles Darwin: Destroyer of Myths. Pen & Sword Books, 2013.

Beatrix Potter: Her Inner World. Pen & Sword Books, 2013.

T.E. Lawrence: Tormented Hero. Fonthill, 2014. *Agatha Christie: The Disappearing Novelist*. Fonthill, 2014.

Lawrence of Arabia's Clouds Hill. Halsgrove, 2014. *Jane Austen: Love is Like a Rose*. Fonthill, 2015. *Kindly Light: The Story of Blind Veterans UK*. Fonthill, 2015.

Thomas Hardy at Max Gate: The Latter Years. Halsgrove, 2016.

Corfe Remembered. Halsgrove, 2017.

Thomas Hardy: Bockhampton and Beyond. Halsgrove, 2017.

Mugabe: Monarch of Blood and Tears. Austin Macauley, 2017

Making Sense of Marilyn. Fonthill, 2018.

Hitler's Insanity: A Conspiracy of Silence. Fonthill, 2018.

The Unwitting Fundamentalist. Austin Macauley, 2018.

Robert Mugabe's Lost Jewel of Africa. Fonthill, 2018.

Hitler: Dictator or Puppet? Pen & Sword, 2011, 2020.

Halsewell: A Shipwreck that Gripped the Nation. Fonthill, 2020.

The Amazing Story of Lise Meitner. Pen & Sword, 2021.

Paul Robeson: A Song For Freedom. New Haven Publishing, 2022

Francoise Hardy: A Musical Tale of Love and Loss. New Haven Publishing, 2022.

Author's website **https://www.andrew**-norman.co.uk And see Andrew Norman Amazon and Amazon Audio.

Index